First World War
and Army of Occupation
War Diary
France, Belgium and Germany

58 DIVISION
Divisional Troops
206 Machine Gun Company
24 October 1916 - 28 February 1918

WO95/2996/10

The Naval & Military Press Ltd
www.nmarchive.com
Published in association with The National Archives

Published by

The Naval & Military Press Ltd

Unit 10 Ridgewood Industrial Park,

Uckfield, East Sussex,

TN22 5QE England

Tel: +44 (0) 1825 749494

www.naval-military-press.com

www.nmarchive.com

This diary has been reprinted in facsimile from the original. Any imperfections are inevitably reproduced and the quality may fall short of modern type and cartographic standards.

© Crown Copyright

Images reproduced by permission of The National Archives, London, England, 2015.

Contents

Document type	Place/Title	Date From	Date To
Heading	WO95/2996/10		
Heading	58th Division No.206 Machine Gun Coy. Mar 1917-1918 Feb		
War Diary	Belton Park Grantham	24/10/1916	09/02/1917
War Diary	Colchester	10/02/1917	10/02/1917
War Diary	Nayland	11/02/1917	14/03/1917
War Diary	Colchester	15/03/1917	15/03/1917
War Diary	Southampton	16/03/1917	17/03/1917
War Diary	Le Havre	18/03/1917	22/03/1917
War Diary	Doullens	23/03/1917	23/03/1917
War Diary	Gaudiempre	24/03/1917	25/03/1917
War Diary	Mondicourt	29/03/1917	13/04/1917
War Diary	Bus	14/04/1917	16/04/1917
War Diary	Achiet-Le-Grand	17/04/1917	24/04/1917
Miscellaneous	O.C. 206 M.G. Company Brigade Major	29/04/1917	29/04/1917
War Diary	Achiet-Le-Grand	24/04/1917	12/05/1917
War Diary	Vaulx-Vraucourt	13/05/1917	20/05/1917
War Diary	Bihucourt	20/05/1917	19/06/1917
War Diary	Ablainzevelle	20/06/1917	30/06/1917
Heading	War Diary Of 206 M.G. Coy From 29/4/17 To 26/5/17		
Miscellaneous	Amendments To 206 M.G. Coy Operation Order No. 6		
Map	Map		
Operation(al) Order(s)	Operation Order No. 6 by Captain L.J.L. Pullar Comdg M.G. Coy		
Miscellaneous	Protective Barrage Fire Table		
Miscellaneous	Amended Machine Gun Barrage Time Table		
Heading	War Diary Of 206 M.G. Coy. From 21/5/17 To 30/6/17 Vol 4		
Heading	War Diary Of 206 M.G. Coy. 1/7/17 To 31/7/17 Vol 5		
War Diary	Ablainzevelle	01/07/1917	08/07/1917
War Diary	Bancourt	09/07/1917	09/07/1917
War Diary	Royaulcourt	10/07/1917	17/07/1917
War Diary	Metz En Coutrue	18/07/1917	31/07/1917
War Diary	Neuville	01/08/1917	01/08/1917
War Diary	Manin	02/08/1917	31/08/1917
Miscellaneous	Barrage Time Table		
Operation(al) Order(s)	Operation Order No. 1		
War Diary	Dambre Camp	01/09/1917	26/09/1917
War Diary	Brake Camp	27/09/1917	30/09/1917
War Diary	Sergeant Thomas Yare	23/09/1917	23/09/1917
War Diary	Corporal John Marriott	23/09/1917	23/09/1917
War Diary	Osmand Philip Pratt	25/09/1917	25/09/1917
War Diary	Sergt Harrison Duncan	25/09/1917	25/09/1917
War Diary	T/Sec. Lieut Arthur Ernest Way	25/09/1917	25/09/1917
War Diary	C.S.M. Ernest Arthur Wigmore	25/09/1917	25/09/1917
War Diary	Private Frederick Edwards	23/09/1917	23/09/1917
War Diary	Reginald Walter Kemp	22/09/1917	22/09/1917
War Diary	Lionel Ernest Howard Whitby	23/09/1917	23/09/1917
Operation(al) Order(s)	206 Machine Gun Co Operation Order No. 11	10/09/1917	10/09/1917

Operation(al) Order(s)	Operation Order No. 12 by Captain L.J.L. Pullar Commanding 206 Machine Gun Company	12/09/1917	12/09/1917
Operation(al) Order(s)	Operation Order No. 14 by Captain L.J.L. Pullar Commanding 206 Machine Gun Company		
War Diary	Autnques	01/10/1917	12/10/1917
War Diary	Autinques	13/10/1917	31/10/1917
Operation(al) Order(s)	Relief Operation Order No. 17	24/10/1917	24/10/1917
Operation(al) Order(s)	Operation Order No. 18 by Captain L.J.L. Pullar Commanding 206 Machine Gun Company	24/10/1917	24/10/1917
Miscellaneous	Operation Report from by Captain L.J.L. Pullar Commanding 206 Machine Gun Company	27/10/1917	27/10/1917
Miscellaneous	Supplementary To Operation Report	27/10/1917	27/10/1917
War Diary	Road Camp Proven Area	01/11/1917	06/11/1917
War Diary	S Camp	07/11/1917	15/11/1917
War Diary	Proven	16/11/1917	26/11/1917
War Diary	Brunembert	27/11/1917	30/11/1917
Operation(al) Order(s)	Operation Order No. 20 by Captain L.J.L. Pullar Commanding 206 Machine Gun Company	05/11/1917	05/11/1917
Operation(al) Order(s)	Operation Order No. 21 by Captain L.J.L. Pullar Commanding 206 Machine Gun Company	10/11/1917	10/11/1917
Operation(al) Order(s)	Operation Order No. 22 by Captain L.J.L. Pullar Commanding 206 Machine Gun Company	11/11/1917	11/11/1917
Miscellaneous	D.M.G.O. 58th Division	12/11/1917	12/11/1917
Miscellaneous	No.1 Daily Report On Firing Work Done Intelligence Summary Tactical Situation	11/11/1917	11/11/1917
Miscellaneous	No.2 Daily Report On Firing Work Done Intelligence Summary Tactical Situation	12/11/1917	12/11/1917
Miscellaneous	No.3 Daily Report On Firing Work Done Intelligence Summary Tactical Situation	13/11/1917	13/11/1917
Operation(al) Order(s)	Operation Order No. 23 by Captain L.J.L. Pullar Commanding 206 Machine Gun Company	14/11/1917	14/11/1917
Operation(al) Order(s)	Operation Order No. 24 by Captain L.J.L. Pullar Commanding 206 Machine Gun Company	25/11/1917	25/11/1917
War Diary	Brunembert	01/12/1917	09/12/1917
War Diary	Mortar Camp	10/12/1917	14/12/1917
War Diary	Kemdton Park	15/12/1917	21/01/1918
War Diary	Cachy	22/01/1918	28/02/1918

NO 95/296/10

58TH DIVISION

NO. 206 MACHINE GUN COY.
MAR 1917 – ~~MAY 1919~~
1918 FEB

Page 1.

Army Form C. 2118.

Vol. I.

WAR DIARY
or
INTELLIGENCE SUMMARY.
(Erase heading not required.)

Place	Date	Hour	Summary of Events and Information	Remarks and references to Appendices
BELTON PARK GRANTHAM.	24.10.16 to 9.2.17		No. 206 M.G. Coy. was mobilised & trained. Attached to C Service Battn., commanded by Lt.-Col. H.F.BIDDER. Strength "A"	
			10 officers, 177 O.R., 57 animals, 13 wagons limbered G.S., 1 water cart, 1 cooks cart, 15 bicycles. Received orders to	
	9.2.17		entrain at GRANTHAM military dock, destination ST BOTOLPH, COLCHESTER	
"	9.2.17	4 p.m.	Entrained at GRANTHAM military dock, 1 casualty during entraining. This man replaced at once by M.G.T.C.	
COLCHESTER	10.2.17	11 p.m.	Arrived ST BOTOLPH station. Detrained & marched to NAYLAND	
NAYLAND	11.2.17 to 14.3.17		Billetted in the private houses. Training proceeded with. Taken on strength of 66th (2nd Line) Division, Battn. Orders Oct. 177 Aust. 14/2/17	
			199th Inf. Bde. Outbreak of German measles 7 casualties. 199th Inf. Bde left for the front 1/3/17. No. Bde. Order W300/W300	
			movement orders received for this coy. Temporarily attached 72nd Bde for rations. Received orders to entrain at	Sd. Army Headqrs
			COLCHESTER NORTH STATION at 10.30 p.m. on 15/3/17 from Southern Army. Also received orders that transport Sd. Army Headqrs	
			must be detrained by 3 officers' horses. Saddlery to be returned to Ordnance, COLCHESTER, horses to BRENTWOOD Sd. Army Letter	
			This done.	
COLCHESTER	15.3.17	10.30 pm	Entrained NORTH station, destination unknown. 8 horses despatched to Southern Army, BRENTWOOD Depôt, including Gen.	
SOUTHAMPTON	16.3.17	5.30 am	Arrived DOCKS station. Detrained & marched up to No. 1 Rest Camp.	
"	17.3.17	11 a.m.	Marched down to docks, & embarked Animals, limbers, & two officers on S.S. COURTFIELD. two & eight officers on	
			S.S. CAESAREA. Destination unknown	
LE HAVRE.	18.3.17	5 am.	Arrived in harbour. Men disembarked, & proceeded to disembark transport from S.S. COURTFIELD. When company complete	

2353 Wt. W2544/1454 700,000 5/15 D. D. & L. A.D.S.S. Forms/C. 2118.

Page 2   Vol I

Army Form C. 2118.

WAR DIARY
or
INTELLIGENCE SUMMARY.
(Erase heading not required.)

Instructions regarding War Diaries and Intelligence Summaries are contained in F.S. Regs., Part II. and the Staff Manual respectively. Title pages will be prepared in manuscript.

Place	Date	Hour	Summary of Events and Information	Remarks and references to Appendices
LE HAVRE	18.3.17	3 p.m.	Marched up to No. 1 Rest Camp.	
"	15.3.17		At No. 1 Rest Camp. All deficiencies replaced. One casualty. Admitted to hospital. One animal a casualty	
"	22.3.17		Through permission Replaced by Remount Dept before our departure	Coy commander orders
"	22.3.17	4 p.m.	Entrained at GARE DES MARCHADISES, Paris 16, destination unknown	
DOULLENS	23.3.17	11 p.m.	Arrived DOULLENS STATION, detrained, & marched to rest camp, for the night. Attached 58th (LONDON) Division	Rec'd wire
GAUDIEMPRE	24.3.17	9 p.m.	Left rest camp, & marched to GAUDIEMPRE, as per Divisional orders; arrived 3 p.m. Billeted in huts	
"			Rationed by 58th Division, & informed that we were Divisional M.G. Coy.	
	24.3.17 to 26.3.17		Training proceeded with.	
	26.3.17		Received orders to march to MONDICOURT on following day, where we would be attached to VII th Corps for Divl service	G.S. 375 Reg. Ord.
			anti-aircraft duty. One Section to be sent to GOUY, one to SAULTY, & one to FOSSEUX, a guard mounting ammunition dumps. Coy H.Q. to be at MONDICOURT, also remaining Section to guard Church there.	
MONDICOURT	29.3.17	3 p.m.	H.Q. & No. 4 Section arrived at LE GROS TISON FARM & billeted in huts. Nos. 1, 2, & 3 Sections marched to SAULTY, GOUY, & FOSSEUX respectively & relieved sections of No. 215 M.G. Coy on anti-aircraft duty.	Section wires
			Relief completed by 6 a.m. satisfactorily. Orders drawn from VII th Corps	
"	30.3.17		Nothing of importance reported. Training tac. No hostile aeroplanes observed.	
"	31.3.17		Nothing of importance to report. Weather & visibility good. No hostile aeroplanes observed.	

2353 Wt. W2544/1454 700,000 5/15 D. D. & L. A.D.S.S.Forms/C 2118.

Page 3.

Army Form C. 2118.

Vol. I

WAR DIARY
INTELLIGENCE SUMMARY.

(Erase heading not required.)

Instructions regarding War Diaries and Intelligence Summaries are contained in F. S. Regs., Part II. and the Staff Manual respectively. Title pages will be prepared in manuscript.

Place	Date	Hour	Summary of Events and Information	Remarks and references to Appendices
MONDICOURT	1.4.17		Nothing of importance reported. No hostile aircraft seen. Visibility & weather good.	
"	2.4.17		Report received from No.1 Section that hostile aeroplane was in the neighbourhood during night. Searchlights were used to, but nothing occurred. All Sections busy building & improving gun platforms etc. General diligence. Weather stormy, with high winds & squalls of rain.	Telephone message from Corps H.Q.
"	3.4.17		No.2 Section reports "Hostile aeroplane passed over at 9.15 a.m flying at great height." Direction S.W. Fire was not opened. All Sections report receipt of Ml.Lt. JACKSON's orders from VIIth Corps H.Q. & were busy instructed in their use. Weather stormy.	
"	4.4.17		No.3 Section reports "Zeppelin reported in neighbourhood about 5 p.m. last night. All lights extinguished & blinds drawn at ViIth Corps H.Q. No hostile aeroplanes seen. Visibility & weather good.	Telephone message from Corps H.Q.
"	5.4.17		No hostile aeroplanes seen. No.2 Section reports "2nd/BEx night-flying commenced 9.0 p.m. Message received from Corps H.Q. last night." Weather very wet.	
"	6.4.17		No hostile aeroplanes seen. No.2 Section reports night-flying by 3rd/BEx. No.3 Section visited by M.G.O. Weather bad.	
"	7.4.17		No.2 Section reports " 1 hostile aeroplane appeared at 10.45 a.m. flying at great height. Fire was opened by Lewis - aircraft guns." Visibility low to moderate. Weather fair. Aeroplanes engaged only by Anti-aircraft guns.	

Page 4

Army Form C. 2118.

Vol. I.

WAR DIARY
INTELLIGENCE SUMMARY.

(Erase heading not required.)

Instructions regarding War Diaries and Intelligence Summaries are contained in F.S. Regs., Part II. and the Staff Manual respectively. Title pages will be prepared in manuscript.

Place	Date	Hour	Summary of Events and Information	Remarks and references to Appendices
MONDICOURT	8.4.17		No hostile aeroplanes seen. Nothing of importance reported. Weather fair.	
"	9.4.17		No 2 Section reports "Two hostile aeroplanes appeared flying at great height at 11.15 a.m. British S.A. They were engaged without result by all four guns". No.1 Section reports "One hostile aeroplane appeared at 11 a.m. but was out of range, so fire was not opened". Visibility moderately clear. Weather good.	
"	10.4.17		No hostile aeroplanes seen. Nothing of importance reported. Weather very wet.	
"	11.4.17		No hostile aeroplanes seen. Nothing of importance reported. Weather very stormy.	
"	12.4.17		No hostile aeroplanes seen. No 2 Section reports night flying by 3 OYSTER last night. Weather very stormy.	
"	13.4.17		No hostile aeroplanes seen. Nothing of importance reported. Weather fair. Orders received from Brown Bay that we would be relieved that night by No.21 M.G.Coy & would proceed to reserve 20 divisions at BUS-LES-ARTOIS. Nos. 1 & 2 Sections together resulted to MONDICOURT at once, & No.3 Section resulted to Armentighieres to BUS the following day after being relieved.	
BUS	14.4.17	2.p.m.	Arrived at Bus from MONDICOURT, complete, with exception of No.3 Section, & regained 53rd Division from Illetta in the village. Orders received from Brown that 214 M.G.Coy would relieve Bus M.G.Coy & that this coy would be attached to 173 2d Inf Bde. Companies to exchange carts harness & hand over maps, correspondence, etc. This done No.3 Section rejoined Coy. from FOSSEUX at 11 h.m. & went	Bde ordr No. J.S.420

2353 Wt. W2544/1451 700,000 5/15 D. D. & L. A.D.S.S. Forms/C. 2118.

Page 5

Army Form C. 2118.

WAR DIARY
Vol. II
or
INTELLIGENCE SUMMARY.
(Erase heading not required.)

Place	Date	Hour	Summary of Events and Information	Remarks and references to Appendices
BUS	14.4.17	11 p.m.	Relief satisfactorily completed and HILL-JACKSON suggest handed over to relieving company.	
"	15.4.17		Day spent in cleaning up, inspecting trenches etc. Weather was wet & cold & roads exceedingly bad owing to mud. One man reported sick & was admitted to field hospital. Orders received from Division to proceed to ACHIET-LE-GRAND on following day & join 173rd Inf. Bde.	
"	16.4.17	9 a.m.	Left BUS for ACHIET-LE-GRAND, via BEAUCOURT, MIRA BEAUMONT HAMEL and MIRAUMONT. Road in good condition, weather fine. Men in good spirits & marching well. No casualties en route.	During G.S. 213
"	"	3 p.m.	Arrived ACHIET-LE-GRAND, & attached 173rd 2/ Inf. Bde. Men in bivouac shelters, officers in tents. Baggage etc. brought on by motor lorry, shared with 175th T.M.B. No G.S. wagon transport can arrive owing to great movements, as we hear, of army transport available when moving. Arrival of nine reinforcements from M.G. Base Depot, our signallers & sixteen gunners. Weather very wet & stormy. Men employed in cleaning up generally, & making shelters as comfortable as possible. Brigade carry out attacks outside ACHIET on the COURCELLES road. Orders received from brigade to put our M.G. detachment as guard against hostile aircraft from building nearby hut and anti-aircraft emplacement at the back of the camp. Four parties detailed to old GERMAN dump at MIRAUMONT to collect timber and corrugated iron, with which to build cook-houses etc. Note of any kind very hard to obtain. Water cart to be sent daily to COURCELLES. This was...	
ACHIET-LE-GRAND	17.4.17			

Page 6 Vol. I

Army Form C. 2118.

WAR DIARY
INTELLIGENCE SUMMARY.

(Erase heading not required.)

Instructions regarding War Diaries and Intelligence Summaries are contained in F. S. Regs., Part II. and the Staff Manual respectively. Title pages will be prepared in manuscript.

Place	Date	Hour	Summary of Events and Information	Remarks and references to Appendices
ACHIET-LE-GRAND	17.4.17		for washing purposes very scarce. Transport also have to go to COURCELLES to water animals. Found in a very bad state owing to heavy rain.	
"	18.4.17		Orders received from Brigade to find working party of 2 Officers & Eighty O.R. for light railway construction work.	BM/227
			Remainder of Company employed throughout the day in building various shelters, cookhouses etc. with material brought from MIRAUMONT. Weather continues wet & stormy. One hostile aeroplane observed. Unable for air to be engaged.	
"	19.4.17		Another working party of two Officers & Eighty O.R. found for light railway construction work. Remainder of Coy employed in building shelters & camouflaging tents. Wire received from Division that gas has been installed in enemy lines at all units in neighbourhood of front line to be on the alert. Weather still bad. No hostile aeroplanes seen.	BM/127 C.R.O. No. V. OF/707 BM/207
"	20.4.17		Another working party of two Officers & Fifty O.R. found for work under R.T.O. at station. One man admitted Field Hospital. One dozen returned from Field Hospital. Weather bad. One hostile aeroplane observed, but too far away, to be engaged.	BM/222
"	21.4.17		Programme of training proceeded with. Weather improving. No hostile aeroplanes seen.	
"	22.4.17		Training proceeded with. A thirty yard range (situated in vicinity of camp. Owing to field hospital Company taken in live-bombing practice by Brigade bombing Officer. Voluntary services held in the evening. One man to field hospital. Two hostile aeroplanes seen, but away for the Weather fine.	
"	23.4.17		Programme of training carried out. One reinforcement arrived from Base Depot & taken on strength. No hostile aeroplanes seen.	
"	24.4.17		Working party of One Officer & Fifty O.R. found for light railway construction work. Recommendation for good work done by the	G.S. 22/17

Army Form C. 348.

...ANDUM.

From O.C. 206 M.G. Company

To Brigade Major

ANSWER.

_____ 29 _____ 1917

Herewith War Diary compiled from date of mobilisation until 28/4/17, as requested.

Duplicate copy is being sent to O i/c M.G.C. Records, 91 York St. Westminster S.W. in accordance with instructions from 3rd Echelon, dated 24/3/17.

(signed) Capt. O.C.
No. 206 M.G. Coy.

WAR DIARY / INTELLIGENCE SUMMARY

Army Form C. 2118. Vol I. Page 7

Place	Date	Hour	Summary of Events and Information	Remarks and references to Appendices
ATHIET-LE(?)ROD	24.4.17		Company sent in to 5th Div by O/c Railway Construction with larger huts to live in, with material brought in from GERMAN DUMP. One man admitted field hospital. No hostile planes seen. Notification received from Brigade that our Brigade was probably going to make a counter-attack to recapture spur of ground running N.E. from VRAUCOURT SUGAR FACTORY, to tgt of Major CORPS who is awaited back. Commanders of units to reconnoitre ground into any other officers they have re clearing.	18/5/42
"	25.4.17		Programme of work carried out. O.C. & two Section Officers on reconnaissance of front line for the Brigade action. New range used by Sections during the day quite successfully. Two hostile planes seen over very low and headed firing. A ground almost struck up. New huts finished, a man moved in. New huts found for men satisfactory.	
"	26.4.17		Programme of work carried out. Second in command & two Section Officers on reconnaissance of front line, and Bde. orders. Range used throughout day. One man to field hospital, one man discharged & reported coy. One hostile plane seen in the distance. Weather found to be in, found in good hard condition. Nothing new of interest or of system found to RTD at station, a employed from up in the midnight.	
"	27.4.17		Company scheme of training carried out. One man rejoined from field hospital. No hostile planes seen. O.C. & T.O. out on reconnaissance for a good route to place of assembly, also Bde. action is counter attack. Weather very fine.	
"	28.4.17		Company scheme of training carried out. No hostile planes seen. Weather very fine.	

Army Form C. 2118.

Page 8.

Vol. I.
WAR DIARY
or
INTELLIGENCE SUMMARY.
(Erase heading not required.)

Instructions regarding War Diaries and Intelligence Summaries are contained in F. S. Regs., Part II. and the Staff Manual respectively. Title pages will be prepared in manuscript.

Place	Date	Hour	Summary of Events and Information	Remarks and references to Appendices
ACHIET-LE-GRAND	29.4.17		Company Scheme of training carried out. One hostile aeroplane seen but too far off. Attack.	
"	30.4.17		Scheme of training carried out. Two hostile aeroplanes seen but not engaged. Weather very fine. All our London fellows with 2nd cont sent for carrying pilot cars full of water, with a view to our advance into hostile territory in the near future. Company held roll. Two hours notice to move into line, to what came be attacked.	
"	1.5.17		Scheme of training carried out. Weather very fine. One man admitted field hospital. Four reinforcements arrived from base depot.	
"	2.5.17		Programme of work carried out. Men engaged in washing clothing & general clean up. One hostile aeroplane passed over, very high up. Weather fine. Notification received of impending British attack on BULLECOURT at dawn the next day. Two limbers requisitioned for duty up in the line. Hostile aeroplane to N.E. of camp during night, dropping bombs. Smell for cloud, probably as result of same. One man returned from field hosp. 21 O.R. men upon ASQUITH's Railway Station N attached 28 Stampede. Brigade scheme of attack practised in conjunction with Infantry. Heavy thumps heard at dawn, evidently British attack on BULLECOURT. Brigade held as Divisional reserve, in case of need. Weather fine but hazy.	
"	3.5.17			
"	4.5.17		Training proceeded with. Weather very fine & dry. No hostile aeroplanes seen.	
"	5.5.17		Programme of events carried out. All ranks put through a gas cloud in the afternoon under practical arrangements. Company held in readiness to move out into horse lines. One man admitted field hospital.	

Army Form C. 2118.

Page 9.

Vol I

WAR DIARY
or
INTELLIGENCE SUMMARY.

(Erase heading not required.)

Instructions regarding War Diaries and Intelligence Summaries are contained in F. S. Regs., Part II. and the Staff Manual respectively. Title pages will be prepared in manuscript.

Place	Date	Hour	Summary of Events and Information	Remarks and references to Appendices
ACHIET-LE-GRAND	6.5.17		Twelve guns with personnel lent to 7th Corps to create barrage to assist 7th Division during attack on BULLECOURT. Guns of Nos. 1, 2, & 3 Sections with their teams moved up same evening to get into position in railway cutting at U.25.b and d (trench Ref BULLECOURT 1/10,000 51.B.S.W. & TRENCH MAP). Our limber (damaged on way up) is halting into shell hole. No. 4 Section remained in camp unit (Coy M.G. Two men injured from shrapnel. Weather very fine.	
"	7.5.17		7th Division attack on BULLECOURT at dawn. Our guns assisted with heavy barrage behind German line. Enemy's shelling of gun position heavy but erratic. No casualties. Our commercial gramophone in no Cats. M.G.O Guns withdrawn some setting & returned to camp. Men shaped well under fire. Although very few had experienced any shelling before. A machine of old pattern, who have been through the worst, in the coming thing possible. Two men admitted field hospital. Weather very hot & dry.	Copies Nos. 134
"	8.5.17		Men resting & cleaning up. Received notice from Brigade that we would probably have to relieve Australian M.G. Coy. to right of BULLECOURT. Then given lent up to NOREUIL to reconnoitre. Day rather warm a strong	
"	9.5.17		Brigade scheme of practicing communication with contact aeroplane carried out & quite successful. Man quite interested. Weather fine. No hostile aeroplanes seen. Gas alarm at midnight, but nothing of importance occurred.	
"	10.5.17		Programme of work carried out. Weather very hot. Winter clothing & blankets being handed in. Instructions received from Brigade that we would be relieving Australians in front of newly captured Hindenburg line in two days time. One man admitted field hospital.	

2353 Wt. W2544/1454 700,000 5/15 D. D. & L. A.D.S.S. Forms/C. 2118.

Army Form C. 2118.

Vol I

WAR DIARY
or
INTELLIGENCE SUMMARY.

Page 10

(Erase heading not required.)

Instructions regarding War Diaries and Intelligence Summaries are contained in F. S. Regs., Part II. and the Staff Manual respectively. Title pages will be prepared in manuscript.

Place	Date	Hour	Summary of Events and Information	Remarks and references to Appendices
ACHIET-LE-GRAND	11.5.17		Programme of work carried out. Weather very hot. C.O and one officer went to NOREUIL with a view to relieving Australians on the night of 12/13 May. Movement Orders issued and all guns and stores prepared for action. Two men admitted to Hospital. Sec Lt Cdr. GILMOUR Transferred from 2nd M.S.Coy and was taken on the strength as supernumerary posted to No 4 Section	
ACHIET-LE-GRAND	12.5.17	10-30 am	Coy fully mobilised marched to near VAUX-VRAUCOURT. Very hot weather. Officers and 4 N.C.O's went ahead to reconnoitre position for us.	
		8 p.m	Taken over from the Australians. Four Sections, four fighting limbers and one other limber parked at 8 pm. Interior delayed for an hour by shelling of VAUX – REVIGNATE Road (R4570 NW). 4 officers and 16 gunners slept behind at Coy HQ (R4)	
VAUX-VRAUCOURT	13.5.17	2 am	[4 mds 5 of VAUX-VRAUCOURT] Relay completed at Rams [casualties 1 OR killed, 2 OR wounded. Four guns placed in Hindenburg front line between C82L-t5 and C28c81 [Nf Ecoust-st-Men 1/40,000]. Two guns in Hindenburg Support Line. Six on Railway Embankment between C5a52 and C2g0 62 [Rf Ecoust-st-Men 1/20,000]. Four guns in Reserve at NOREUIL. Heavy shelling of front line which]	
		3 am	Trenches very fully	
			made Elmarot 3 am. Enemy infantry attack dissipated. Distributed shelling Ampiete follows. Prisoners	
		6 pm	Knocked about but no gun emplacements affected. Casualties 1 OR killed, 3 OR wounded. Coy HQK established on Railway Embankment. Weather very stormy. Co-operation effected in front with Australian Battn on Right flank.	
VAUX VRAUCOURT	14.5.17		Another fine. Enemy shelled avalanche (environs of Frontline Trench, Supports, Reserve, and Communication trenches from NOREUIL, which developed into an intense barrage on the front line at 6 pm when bombardment bombwalls such 4 am the night day when barrage lifted on to support lines. Great difficulty was experienced in getting Rations and water up to the front line from NOREUIL. Enemy sniping very active. An officer and 5 gunners of First QMS WIGMORE from 11 p.m. until 3 am the following day. The QMS gt. successfully organised his Ration party under Shell	

2353 Wt. W2544/1454 700,000 5/15 D. D. & L. A.D.S.S. Forms/C. 2118.

WAR DIARY
INTELLIGENCE SUMMARY

Army Form C. 2118.

Place	Date	Hour	Summary of Events and Information	Remarks and references to Appendices
VAUX-VRAUCOURT	14.5.17		Trying circumstances, and got back with no casualties. He alone was sent forward for an award, in that he masterly man the Brigade who gathered a Lewis party up in Bullecourt. Capt. Zm. J.C. MURLEY M.C. O.C. Coy 2nd was wounded in the evening while attempting to reach the front line and 2nd Lt P. RICHARDS slightly wounded in the arm, the however remained at his post in the front line trenches. Casualties for the day upto 6 p.m. 1 Bomber 5 O.R. wounded. 2 O.R. wounded.	
VAUX-VRAUCOURT	15.5.17	4 a.m.	Enemy barrage lifted from front line K. Support line, and enemy attacked in writing formation. Enemy's strength was estimated to be... The three two m.m. guns of this Company, who had known the boundaries between our post of action in support of Railway Sap, they cut, persuaded our Coy employed the surviving trench. One of the central guns has a temporary stoppage due to a broken sniper sight, a section repairing the gun and crew were put out of action by an enemy bombing party of 1 officer and 3 men. It attack was successfully repulsed and was further attempt was made by the enemy. Shortly afterwards, at H.S. PRIESTLEY on the Railway Embankment and 2nd Lt C.H. GILMOUR on the front line was wounded, the latter by the bombing party mentioned above. Casualties on the day up to 6 a.m. 2 officers wounded 1 O.R. wounded. 10 O.R. Died of wounds. In the sup. front line, one gun was put out of action by shell fire. At noon the 2nd in command [Lt H.M. DUFFIELD] carried up to Advanced Coy HQ and took over command of the day all three arrangements was made for an into Company Relief on through of the 15th/16th N°1 Section relieve 11th N°3 Section in Mr. Support. N°3 Section from three has had Lewis charge with N°3 Section in Mr. Support line, N°4 Section	

Army Form C. 2118.

Vol I

WAR DIARY

INTELLIGENCE SUMMARY.

Page 12

(Erase heading not required.)

Instructions regarding War Diaries and Intelligence Summaries are contained in F. S. Regs., Part II. and the Staff Manual respectively. Title pages will be prepared in manuscript.

Place	Date	Hour	Summary of Events and Information	Remarks and references to Appendices
VAULX-VRAUCOURT	15.5.17		Going down into Reserve at NOREUIL. Thos Relief was carried out with no casualties. Total Casualties for day 2 offs wounded, 1 O.R. died of wounds, 13 O.R. wounded. Went up to the Sp—— operations carried out & was found that the stationary barrage was very satisfactory, and the establishment of trades & P.n. on the front line in the rear would have necessitated the employment of many more guns and thus increased the chances of casualties. Too much stress cannot be laid on the necessity for the proper adjustment of muzzle caps. The Coy were congratulated by the Brigadier on its effectiveness of fire.	
VAULX-VRAUCOURT	16.5.17		Enemy retaliation except for snipers nil 7pm. Reconnoitres of parties reported enemy trenches clear, but at 7 pm, an enemy post was brought on our front line until 7.45 pm. No attack developed. Casualties Nil. Th Water Supply on the front line trench was successfully carried out by means of petrol cans. There was rumour from Snipers.	
VAULX VRAUCOURT	17.5.17		Weather fine. Desultory shelling of front, support and reserve lines all day. Casualties 1 O.R. wounded.	
VAULX VRAUCOURT	18.5.17		Weather fine. Enemy Very inactive except for Snipers and authorities trench from his front lines. Heavy trench weapons this Coy in Bde Reserve lines. Casualties Nil.	
VAULX-VRAUCOURT	19.5.17		Weather fine. Enemy artfully inactive throughout the manoeuvres than the previous day. The Company were relieved tonight by the 141st Bn 215 M.G. Company. Relief complete by 3.30 am. Casualties 3 O.R. Since 3 Bd. Seen used against our ⟨to⟩ 215 M.G. Coy and only guns, tripods and gun accessories brought out. The company proceeded to BIHUCOURT (R/kind SB 57.44W).	
BIHUCOURT	20.5.17	12 noon	BIHUCOURT when it rested for 3 hours, and then marched to its camp at BIHUCOURT (R/kind SB 57.44W).	

WAR DIARY or INTELLIGENCE SUMMARY

Army Form C. 2118.

Page 13

Place	Date	Hour	Summary of Events and Information	Remarks and references to Appendices
BIHUCOURT	20.5.17		The total casualties of the Coy during the return were Major 4 Officers wounded, 27 wounded (4 of whom died of wounds), 3 O.R. wounded in taken prisoners in the day. The company with the rest of the Brigade were congratulated by the corps and division on its stubborn defence and adherence to its lines even though so to have more than four gun numbers in that position, as there were no dug outs for the bruces and no frames if more than four men not only unnecessary but received the thanks of Casualties. One man admitted to hospital in the day.	
BIHUCOURT	21.5.17		Company resting. Wrote out C.S.M. Donaldson reported for duty from 190th M.G. Coy. 2nd Lt Tan Walker and 3rd Pl. held stars on a M.G. course. Wrote [struck out]	
BIHUCOURT	22.5.17		Programme of work carried out. Wrote for. Company rifting and cleaning up. 1 O.R. admitted Hospital.	
BIHUCOURT	23.5.17		Programme of work carried out. Wrote for. Inspection of 11th sec. Transport by Brigadier. 1 O.R. proceeded on leave U.K. 2 O.R. admitted Hospital. 1 O.R. discharged from Hospital. 2nd Lt Penman R.A., 2nd Lt Boyd M.H.S., 2nd Lt Pratt O.R. reposted from M.G. Base Depot and now posted to No 2, 3, 4 Sections respectively. A draft of 29 O.R. also reported and was taken on the strength.	
BIHUCOURT	24.5.17		Wrote for. Programme of work carried out. 1 O.R. discharged from Hospital.	
do	25.5.17		Wrote fine. Programme of work carried out. Transport inspected by Brigadier. 2 O.R. reported from hospital.	
do	26.5.17		Wrote fine. Programme of work carried out. Inspection of horses by O.C. Divl Train.	

WAR DIARY or INTELLIGENCE SUMMARY

Army Form C. 2118.

Vol 1. Page 14

Place	Date	Hour	Summary of Events and Information	Remarks and references to Appendices
BIHUCOURT	27.5.17		Avalakfur. Inspection of Transport and Armoury by Brigadier Gen. B.C. Freyberg, V.C. D.S.O. Bn also formed into 4 Rest Camp.	
"	28.5.17		Weather fine. Programme of work carried out. 173rd Bde. relieved 185th Bde. in Sector N of BULLECOURT. Capt. L.J. Fallon took over command of the Coy. vice Capt. J.C. Hunting M.C. wounded.	
"	29.5.17		Weather fine and dull. Camp at BIHUCOURT broken up. Coy. moved up to MORY ridge, push on along to relieving No. 205 M.G. Coy. x No. 206 M.G. Coy. in sector N of BULLECOURT. from ECOUST to CROISILLES.	
"	30.5.17		Relief carried out successfully. No casualties. Weather fine. Nos. 1, 2 and 3 Sections holding line of railway embankment. Two Guns of No. 3. Section manning line guns of No. 206 Coy., left in until defence of ECOUST and to rather assist by No. 214. Coy. Enemy quiet except for occasional shelling of ECOUST cemetery.	
"	31.5.17		Our artillery opened barrage fire at 3.45 a.m. on enemy front line along front held by this brigade. Fire ceased at 3.55 a.m. Hostile artillery opened 3.58 a.m. & ceased at 4.00 a.m. No barrage identified. Intermittent shelling with 5.9 offhand. Enemy shells included large percentage Glands. Defence of ECOUST taken over by No. 214 Coy. with exception of Nos. 8 and 10 guns, which are provided by No. 1 Section. Two teams of No. 3 Section and guns of No. 205 Coy. therefore in the air. Two O.R. wounded (One remained at duty).	
"	1.6.17		Front normal. Hostile Artillery. Our artillery active between 7 p.m and 7.30 p.m; also active between 2.20 a.m and 3 a.m. Aeroplane observed hit by shell fire at 4.45 a.m. and below descended in our lines. Work done A+B Gun emplacements reconstructed.	
"	2.6.17		Front quiet. Hostile Artillery normal. Enemy sent up S.O.S. and did not get any reply for 15 minutes, and then sent over only about 5. One man admitted to hospital.	
"	3.6.17		Front normal. Enemy Artillery active at intervals. ECOUST U.26 a and b shelled at 11 p.m and 2 a.m and cutting from U.25 f 6.3 to U 21.2.6.6 traversed by enemy artillery. Our aircraft extremely active. One enemy aeroplane observed at 4 a.m out of range of any of our machine guns.	

WAR DIARY or INTELLIGENCE SUMMARY

Army Form C. 2118.

Instructions regarding War Diaries and Intelligence Summaries are contained in F.S. Regs., Part II. and the Staff Manual respectively. Title pages will be prepared in manuscript.

(Erase heading not required.)

Place	Date	Hour	Summary of Events and Information	Remarks and references to Appendices
	4.6.17		Front throughout the day quiet. Very little shelling by enemy during day; intermittent during night. Our own artillery lively. Aircraft very busy throughout day. Some hostile planes than usual came over. Twelve advanced at 8.30 p.m. out of range of our guns. There was no machine gun action on our part.	
	5.6.17		Front normal. Artillery on both sides moderate. Several words lively. Several hostile machines went over Enemy's own lines about 8.30 p.m. Hostile machine brought down in our lines by aircraft first sighted by front line infantry. Aviators were removed under cover of darkness. Our own machine guns were used to [patrolling?].	
	6.6.17		Front throughout the day quiet. Hostile and own artillery on the whole normal. Our trench mortars did not fire. No 4 Section relieved No 5 Section. A detachment of No 3 Section took over new gun positions at U.13 d 5.5. Established R.E. dump at U.25 a.4.8.	
	7.6.17		Front quiet. Our artillery active throughout day and night. At 4.50 a.m. the hostile planes flew over our lines but were beaten off by our anti-aircraft guns. No hostile men seemed out during the day by our own guns. 2 men from Bois depot taken in strength. One man discharged from hospital and rejoined.	
	8.6.17		Front generally quiet. Own artillery active throughout day. Enemy put down two Barrages on our posts lasting from 9.45 p.m. to 10.15 p.m. chiefly light Minen. No apparent reason for this, as no movement on our part was observed.	
	9.6.17		Front quiet on the whole. Own artillery active. At 11.25 p.m. we put down Barrage on Enemy front line. Carried out a raid. Enemy retaliated slightly with 5.9s - fairly violent. Fire slackened down to normal at 12.10 p.m. Sufft ammunition dumped. Our machine guns did not fire. One man admitted to F. Hospital. One N.C.O. proceeded on Course. 2nd Lt Walker and 308 returned from Course.	

Army Form C. 2118.

WAR DIARY
or
INTELLIGENCE SUMMARY.
(Erase heading not required.)

Page 16

Place	Date	Hour	Summary of Events and Information	Remarks and references to Appendices
	10.6.17		Front quiet generally. Our own Artillery active throughout whole day. Except for rather heavy shelling at 7.30 p.m. chiefly on our front line, enemy guns silent. The Company Machine Guns did not fire. Honours:- Captain J.C. MURLEY awarded Bar to M.C.; 2nd Lieut P. RICHARDS awarded M.C.; 63633 Sergt. S. BEDFORD awarded D.C.M. all for action on 15.5.1917.	
	11.6.17		Front quiet on the whole. Our Artillery active all day. Enemy put down barrage on our front line from 7.30 p.m. until 8.0 p.m. Our Machine Guns did not fire.	
	12.6.17		Front quiet. Our Artillery very active throughout day and night. Enemy Artillery quiet. Our Machine Guns did not fire. All Machine Guns Emplacements improved, and also dug outs for teams. A this machine Emplacement sited and under construction. One Dug out made for Coy H.Q. at 10 Trees.	
	13.6.17		Front normal. Enemy Artillery quiet generally. Our Artillery active between 11.45 & 12.15 a.m. and afterwards at intervals. From 3.0 a.m. until 3.12 a.m. intense bombardment by our artillery. Some French retaliation by enemy, a lot of shells dropped short, but did not burst. Our Machine Guns did not fire.	
	14.6.17		Front quiet. Own Artillery active. Enemy Artillery quiet throughout the day. From 2.10 a.m. until 2.45 a.m. he put down barrage on our front line, apparently in answer to S.O.S. Signal but own party and our Machine Guns did not fire.	
	15.6.17		Attack made upon the Hindenburg Line - Escaut Sector - by 173rd Infantry Brigade assisted by the C.5 Machine Guns. One Section of 4 Guns were allotted to 2/5 Bn. London Regt. on left, one Section of whom to Batts. on Right, and Eight Guns placed upon own main line of defence i.e. along Railway Cutting and Sunken Road. At 2.50 a.m. These 8 Guns opened an indirect barrage fire in conjunction with Artillery & continued until the latters fire slackened. During action 6 of the advanced guns reached their objective. Two guns were sent up to reinforce. Four Guns were lost during action. During day Guns on the Sunken Road & Railway Cutting put down sharp bursts of fire at frequent intervals. Enemy put down a heavy barrage on our Front Line from 7 p.m. to 7.30 p.m. Casualties:- Officers: 2nd Lieut R.A. OREY, killed; 2nd Lieut R.A. PERMAN killed; 2nd Lieut T.R. WATKER wounded; 2nd Lieut W.A. STUART-BOYD wounded; Other Ranks 2 killed; 5 missing; 1 wounded + missing; 3 wounded.	

Army Form C. 2118.

WAR DIARY
or
INTELLIGENCE SUMMARY.

(Erase heading not required.)

Instructions regarding War Diaries and Intelligence Summaries are contained in F. S. Regs., Part II. and the Staff Manual respectively. Title pages will be prepared in manuscript.

Place	Date	Hour	Summary of Events and Information	Remarks and references to Appendices
	16/6/17	1.45 a.m.	Heavy Barrage put down by our Machine Guns, & own Artillery, lasting for 20 minutes. Machine Guns at Railway cutting fired frequent bursts throughout the day. Enemy Artillery active. Casualties O. Ranks. 1 killed; 11 wounded.	
	17/6/17		Front fairly quiet. Our own Artillery active at intervals. Enemy Artillery heavily shelled our lines between 8.30 p.m. & 9 p.m. Our Machine Guns fired at intervals. Casualties O. Ranks:- 3 killed; 1 Died of Wounds; 6 wounded. Company relieved by 2/5 Machine Gun Coy.	
	18/6/17		Company resting. Weather fine with occasional storms.	
	19/6/17		Inspection of Stores & kits. Weather fair with showers.	
ABLAINZEVELLE	20/6/17		Company left Army Ridge for Ablainzevelle. Busy building shelters. Weather fine. (ABLAINZEVELLE)	
"	21/6/17		Company completed construction of shelters. Weather showery.	
"	22/6/17		Gun stores etc. checked. Weather fine.	
"	23/6/17		A working party of 1 N.C.O & 30 men found for general repair work at R.F.C. Ground on Ingoyenville Road. Weather beautiful. One O.R. returned from Hospital.	
"	24/6/17		Programme of work carried out. Weather fair.	
"	25/6/17		Programme of work carried out. Divisional Machine Guns Officer inspected Company at work. One man proceeded to Rest Camp. Two men returned from Rest Camp. Weather fine.	

WAR DIARY
or
INTELLIGENCE SUMMARY

Army Form C. 2118.

Page 19

Place	Date	Hour	Summary of Events and Information	Remarks and references to Appendices
ABLAINZEVELLE	26/6/17		Programme of work carried out. Reinforcements. Following officers reported this day. 2nd Lieut J.A. Tomlinson, 2nd Lieut J.R. Walker; 2nd Lieut W. Pitksure from Base Depot. Weather dull.	
"	27/6/17		Programme of work carried out. Weather fine.	
"	28/6/17		Programme of work carried out. A draft of 1 N.C.O + 32 O. Ranks reported this day from Base Depot. Weather stormy.	
"	29/6/17		Programme of work carried out. Weather fine.	
"	30/6/17		Programme of work carried out. 1 N.C.O returned from M.G. Course at Camiers. 1 N.C.O left for M.G. Course. 3 men admitted to Hospital. Weather wet.	

58th Div.

Vol 3

CONFIDENTIAL
****

WAR DIARY

OF

206 M.C. Coy.

From 20/4/17
To... 29/5/17

SECRET

War Diary

AMENDMENTS TO 175th I.B.
OPERATION ORDER No 6

Para 1 will now read:-

PLAN The 175th Infantry Brigade assisted by the 174th Infantry Brigade is to carry out an attack on the HINDENBURG line in relief of the line.

The attack will be made on ..... of the 2 Sep and 2040 hours will be Zero Hour.

Troops on our right and left are co-operating in the attack ...... part of ..... our fire ..... will .... coinciding ...... Zero]

The Objects of the attack are :-
(a) To gain ground, to threaten ...... and [?]
(b) To improve our tactical positions.
(c) To take prisoners.

Para 2 will now read :- OBJECTIVES

1st Objective   HINDENBURG front line from U26 b 60 7 to U14 a 40 45
2nd Objective   HINDENBURG support line from U20 b 45 70 to U14 a 5 ?

Para 7 will now read :-

SCHEME OF ATTACK

The Brigade will attack with the 2/5th Bn London Regiment on the Right, 2/6th Bn London Regt in the centre, and the 2/8th Bn

London Regt on the Right

The 2/5th, 2/6th and 2/2nd Bn London Regts will attack on a four Company front

C Company from the 2/7th & 2/8th Bns will be attached to the 2/5th & 2/6th Bns respectively, and will be given the task of making good our flanks.

The attack will be launched in two waves. Moppers will accompany the first wave.

First Wave of each Company will consist of two Platoons in single Rank. One platoon per Company will follow the first wave at 10 paces distance to act as Moppers.

Second Wave will be 50 paces distance from the first wave and will consist of one Platoon per each Battn. Light Trench Mortar Personnel with their L.T.M. Bombs and will follow the first wave & will move alongside of the Battn, one near the two specified Coys.

The Advance & Assault. The whole assaulting force will move forward at once and get close up to the Barrage.

Great care should be exercised:-
(a) To maintain the distances laid down.
(b) To lose no chance of reorganisation during advance.
(c) To use compasses whenever distance occurs, even when waiting a few seconds for the barrage to lift (Aim to rally)

The second wave will advance at 50 paces distance from the first wave after the first objective, when they will mop up the Sunken Road

hold any places between the first and
second objectives. They will then push
forward into the second objective and will
assist with mopping up and consolidation.

Para 8 will now read — SPECIAL DETACHMENTS

O's C 2/7th & 2/5th Bns will detail the
Companies attached to them from 1/5th & 2/7th
Bns to form Left & Right Defensive flanks
respectively, as shown on Map.

Para 9 will now read —

VICKERS MAXIM GUNS

The advance will be supported by the
Guns of the 2/1st, 2/2nd & the MG Coy and
the Teams of the 3rd Division. C.O. 2/1st M.G.
Coy will arrange for 2 teams to follow the
second waves of each Company of the 2/3rd
2/1st & 2/2nd Bns. These guns will occupy
the nearest positions in the first objective
during hostile bombardment and will
fire over the heads of our men in the second
objective during a counter attack. The
remainder of the guns will employ indirect
fire under the orders of O/c 2/1st M.G. Co.

Para 10 will now read — LIGHT TRENCH MORTARS

O.C. 173rd L.T.M. Battery will detail his
personnel equally to the 2/3rd, 2/1st & 2/2nd
Bns to act as special moppers up detailed
in para 7. He will be responsible that

they are handed over fully equipped
MACHINE GUNS OF 208 M.G. COY will now
read :- Machine Guns of 206 Coy will
co-operate as follows :-
(1) Indirect Barrage Fire
(2) Indirect Fire by forward
guns over troops in
HINDENBURG Support Line
to assist in repelling hostile
counter attack

"A" Front Line Section will be kept
along Embankment to act as Garrison
Guns. These Guns will not move forward
but continue to employ an Indirect
S.O.S. Concentration Fire

A Sub Section will be allotted
to each of the following Bns 2/1st, 2/2nd
& 2/3rd and will follow the advance
wave of each Company of these Bns.
These Guns will occupy the MEBUS
position at first objective during
Hostile Bombardment but will fire
over heads of our own men in the
Second Objective during counter
attack.

These Guns will be allotted to Bns
as follows :-
4 K Guns under 2/Lt W.K. Stuart Roy
to the 2/2nd Battalion on Left

C & D Guns under 2/Lt Thrustall to the 2/L Bn on Centre.

One Lt Section only – 1 and 2 Guns of No 1 Section, under 2/Lt Leahy, to the 3rd Battalion on Right.

One Lt Section viz 3 and 4 Guns of No 1 Section will be held in Reserve along the bank and will be prepared to reinforce any Battalion Sector at a moment's notice.

Coy O/C Officers will forward guides requiring reinforcement, and such a guide in order to prevent late reinforcement arriving at positions.

Guns H, E, G & K, under 2nd Lt R.F. Kemp and 2/Lt H.K. Talbot, will be detailed as Garrison Guns and will not move forward.

Guns F, J, A & B under 2/Lt R.A. Pemman & 2/Lt O.P. Pratt will assist Garrison Guns in Barrage Fire but must be prepared to move forward by Gun Teams to any Sector to replace unexpected Casualties.

The Artillery & Machine Gun Barrage Time Table is circulated and amended Gun attached.

4. The Indirect Overhead Fire Table
is amended as follows -

Barrage Guns lay on to original
targets & then elevate 100° without firing
at ZERO they fire at this elevation in
accordance with amended Time Table
attached

Section officers of forward Guns will
report to OC Battalion of their respective
Sectors 21.00 19/6/17

Advanced Report Centre
U 19 d 7 5 6 5.

Telephone Stations etc
U 25 a 7 5 5 0
T 24 d 8 2

Power Buzzer at Advanced Report Centre
set a place to be notified later

Wireless
T 24 d 6 2

Visual Station
U 19 b 6 0 5 5
T 24 d 6 2
T 30 c 7 9

L. H. Pullan
Captain
O/C 206 M.G. Coy

Copies sent to
1. 173 Infantry Brigade
2.
3.
4.
5.
6.
7.
8.

SECRET   War Diary

AMENDMENTS TO 206 M G Co
OPERATION ORDER No 6

Para 1 will now read:-

PLAN - The 173rd Infantry Brigade, supported by the 174th Infantry Brigade is to carry out an attack on the HINDENBURG Front and Support Lines

The attack will be made by moonlight Z day and ZERO hour will be issued later.

Troops on our Right and Left will co-operate with rifle, machine gun and Lewis Gun fire, and will undertake minor operations as outlined in para 7.

The objects of the attack are:-
(a) To gain ground, to kill and harass the enemy
(b) To improve our tactical position
(c) To take prisoners.

Para 2 will now read:- OBJECTIVES.

1st Objective HINDENBURG Front Line from U 20 b 40 17 to U 14 a. 05 05

2nd Objective. HINDENBURG SUPPORT LINE from U 20 b 45 72 to U 14 a 8 1.

Para 7 will now read:-

SCHEME OF ATTACK

The Brigade will attack with the 2/3rd Bn London Regiment on the Right 2/1st Bn London Regt in the centre, and the 2/2nd Bn

London Regt on the Left

The 2/3rd, 2/1st and 2/2nd Bn London Regts will attack on a four Company front.

A Company from the 2/7 & 2/8 Bns, will be attached to the 2/3rd & 2/2nd Bns respectively and will be given the task of making good our flanks.

The attack will be launched in two waves. Moppers will accompany the front wave.

First Wave of each Company will consist of two platoons in Single Rank. One platoon per Company will follow the first wave at 10 paces distance to act as Moppers.

Second Wave will be 30 paces distance from the front wave and will consist of one Platoon.

Special Moppers. Light Trench Mortar Personnel, with three L T M Bombs each, will follow the front wave to deal with dug out shafts, which are near the Enemy's Support Line.

The Advance & Assault. The whole assaulting force will move forward at Zero and get close up to the Barrage.

Great care should be exercised –

    (a) To maintain the distances laid down
    (b) To lose no chance of reorganisation during advance.
    (c) To use compasses whenever advance occurs, even when waiting a few seconds for the barrage to lift (This is vital).

The second wave will advance at 30 paces distance from the first wave after the first objective, when they will mop up the Sunken Road

and any places between the first and
second objectives. They will then push
forward into the second objective and will
assist with mopping up and consolidation.

Para 8 will now read. SPECIAL DETACHMENTS

O.C. 2/2nd & 2/3rd Bns will detail the
Companies attached to them from 2/4 & 2/7th
Bns to form Left & Right defensive flanks
respectively as shown on Map

Para 9 will now read :-

VICKERS MAXIM GUNS

The advance will be supported by the
Guns of the 201, 195 & 214 M.G. Coys and
the Guns of the 21st Division. O.C. 206 M.G.
Coy will arrange for 2 Guns to follow the
second waves of each Company of the 2/3rd
2/1st & 2/2nd Bns. These guns will occupy
the nebus positions in the first objective
during hostile bombardments but will
fire over the heads of our men in the second
objective during a counter attack. The
remainder of the guns will employ indirect
fire under the orders of O/C 206 M.G.

Para 10 will now read - LIGHT TRENCH MORTARS

O.C. 173rd L.T.M Battery will detail his
personnel equally to the 2/3rd, 2/1st & 2/2nd
Bns to act as special mappers as detailed
in para 7. He will be responsible that

they are handed over fully equipped

MACHINE GUNS OF 206 M.G. Coy will now read - Machine Guns of 206 Coy will Co-operate as follows -

with   (1) Indirect Barrage Fire
          (2) Indirect Fire by forward guns over troops in HINDENBURG Support Line to assist in repelling hostile counter attack.

At least one Section will be kept along Embankment track as Garrison Guns & these Guns will not move forward but continue to employ an Indirect S.O.S. Concentration Fire.

A Sub Section will be allotted to each of the following Bns 2/1st, 2/2nd & 2/3rd and will follow the second waves of each Company of these Bns. These Guns will occupy the MEBUS position in first objective during hostile bombardment but will fire over heads of our own men in the Second objective during a counter attack.

These Guns will be allotted to Bns as follows -

J & K Guns under 2/Lt W.K. Stuart Ryl to the 2/2nd Battalion on Left

C & D Guns under 2/Lt Tankerville to the 2/1st Bn. on Centre.

One Sub Section viz — 1 and 4 Guns of No 1 Section under 2/Lt Rabley to the 2/5th Battalion on Right.

One Sub Section viz — 2 and 3 Guns of No 1 Section will be held in Reserve along Embankment & be prepared to reinforce any Battalion Sector at a moment's notice.

Any M.G. officer with forward guns requiring a reinforcement must send a guide in order to facilitate reinforcement arriving at position.

Guns (H)(E)(S) & (10) under Second Lt R.V. Kemp and 2/Lt H.R. Waldock will be detailed as Garrison Guns and will not move forward.

Guns (F)(G)(A)(B) under 2/Lt R.A. Pennens & 2/Lt O.P. Pratt will assist Garrison Guns in Barrage Fire but must be prepared to move forward by Gun Teams to any Sector to replace unexpected Casualties.

The artillery & Machine Gun Barrage Time Table is cancelled and amended ones attached.

The Indirect Overhead Fire Table

is amended as follows -

Barrage Guns lay on to original targets + then elevate 100° without firing at ZERO they fire at this elevation in accordance with Amended Time Table attached.

Section officers of Forward Guns will report to OC Battalion of their respective Sectors 2100 10/6/17

Advanced Report Centre

U.19. b. 7. 5. 6. 5

Telephone Stations etc

U 25 a. 7. 5. 5. 0
T 24 d. 8. 2

Power Buzzer at Advance Report Centre + at a place to be notified later

Wireless

T 24 d 5 2

Visual Station

U 19 b 6 0 5 5
T 24 d 8 2
T 30 c 7 9

L J H Pedlar
Captain
O/C 206 M.C. Coy

Copies sent to:-
1. 173 Infantry Brigade
2. By Pounder Tr. Battn.
3. 214   55   D10 50
4. Wireless
5. "
6. 4 Ind Guns
7. " "
8. HES.10.
9. FGAB
10. M.G. Sections

SCALE 1:2,500. Reference 51&SW. SQUARE "U". C.J.Graham.
OPERATION MAP No 4(a) 2/Lt.

E= Entrance to Dugout Gallery or M.G. emplacement on parapet.

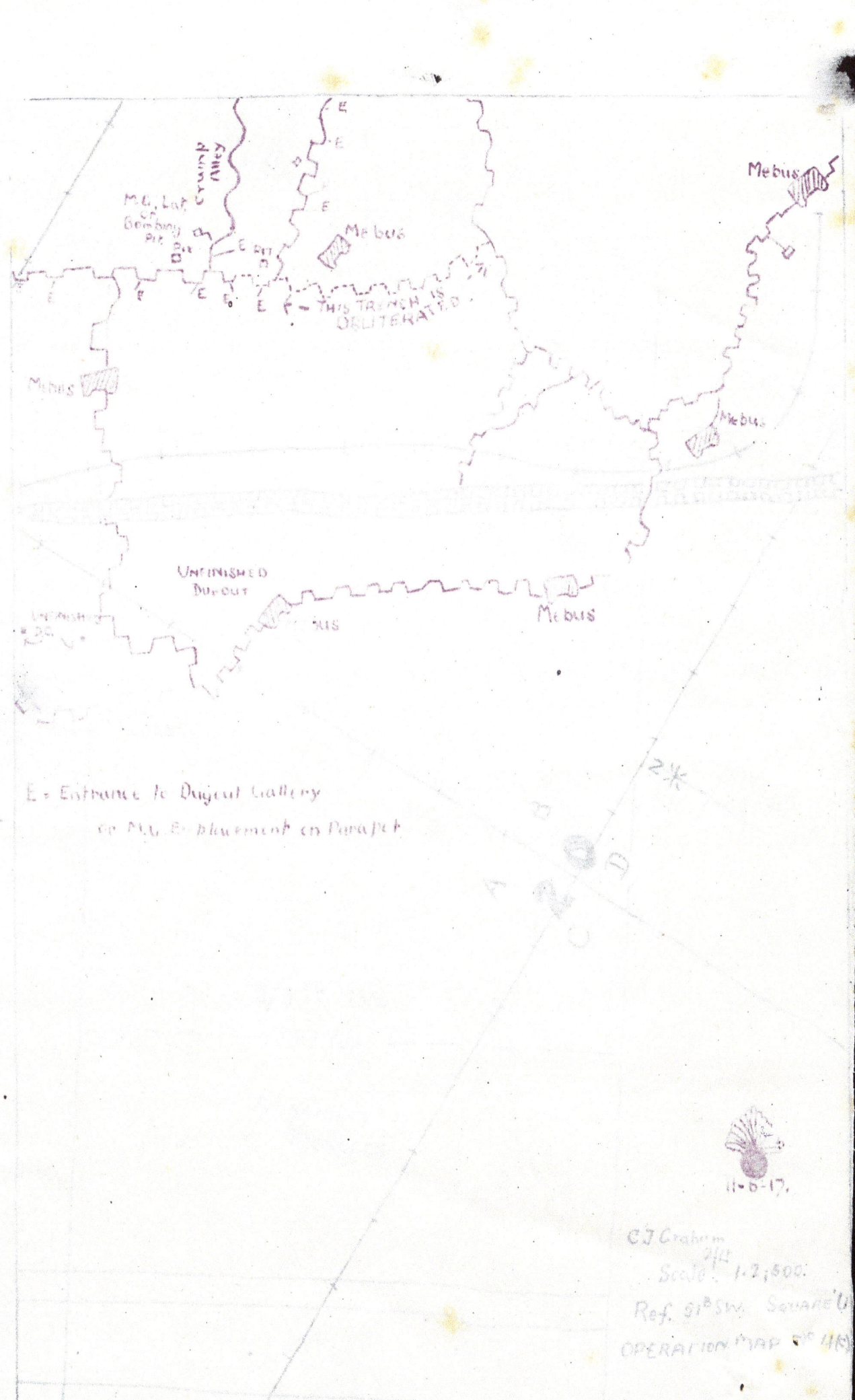

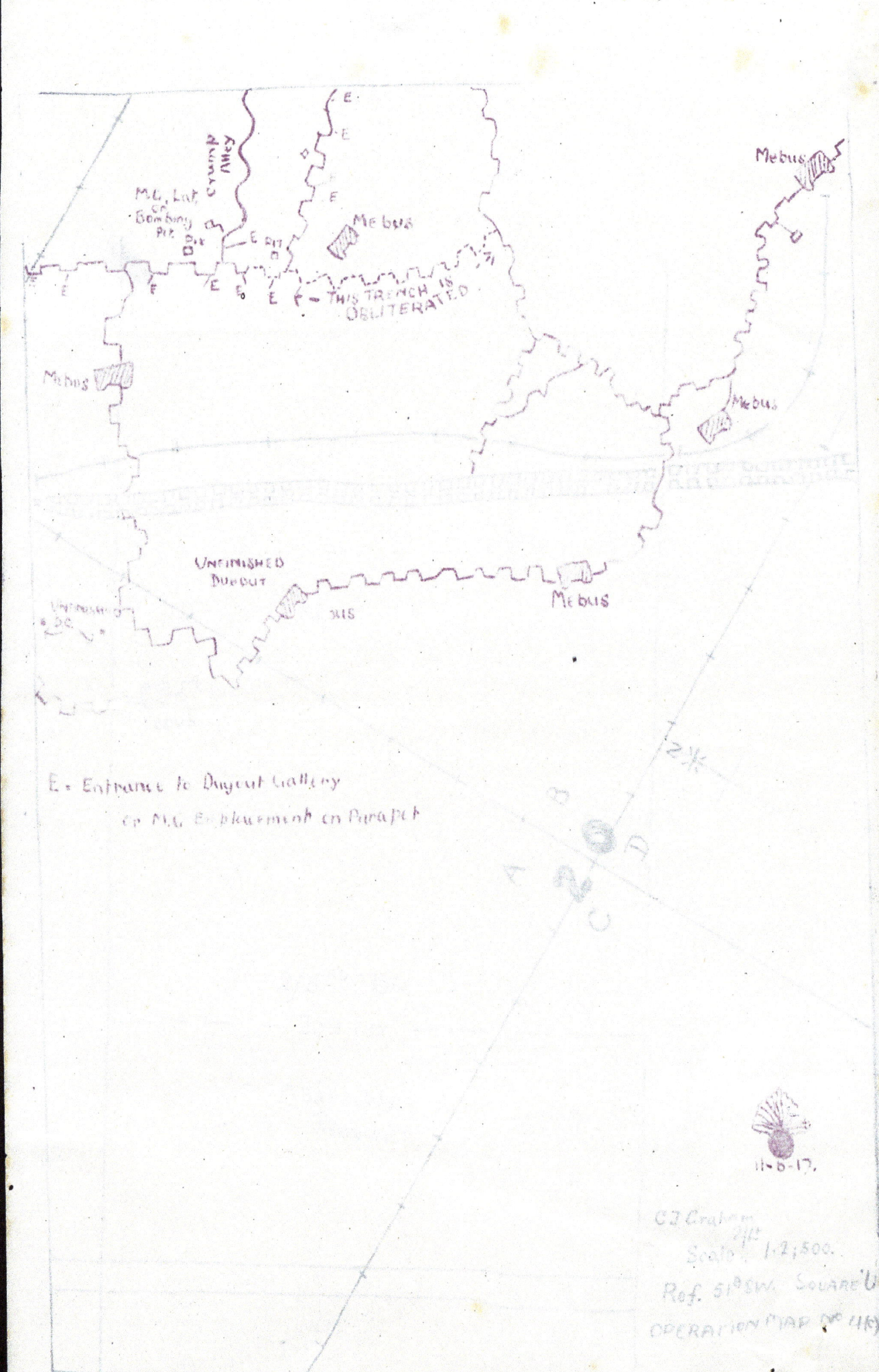

Crump Alley

M.G. Lat. or Bombing Pit. Dug.

E PIT

Mebus

THIS TRENCH IS OBLITERATED

Mebus

Mebus

UNFINISHED DUGOUT

UNFINISHED D.C.

M.S.

Mebus

Mebus

E = Entrance to Dugout Gallery
or M.G. Emplacement on Parapet

11-D-17.

C.J. Graham
2/Lt
Scale: 1:2,500.
Ref. 51°SW. Square
OPERATION MAP. No. 118

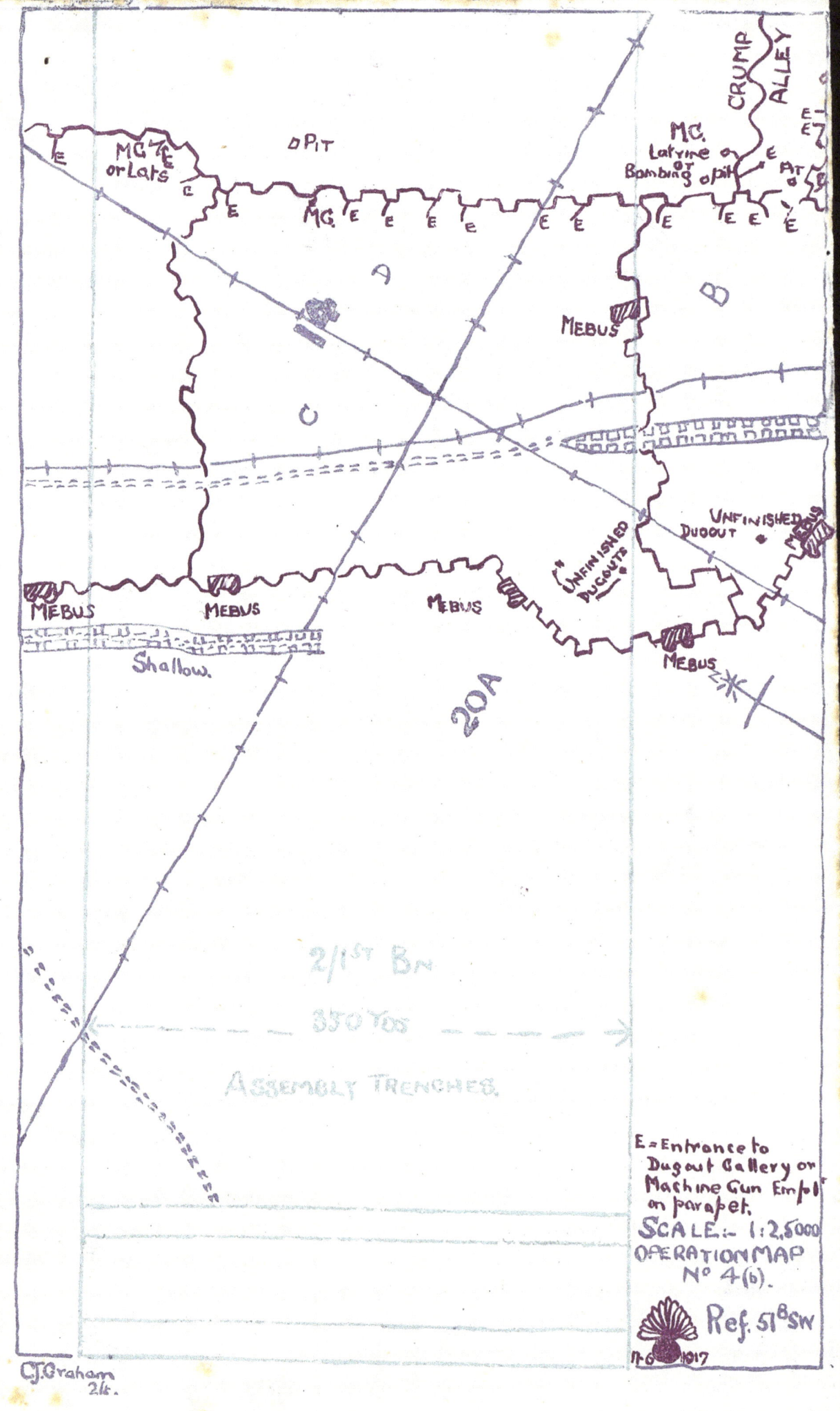

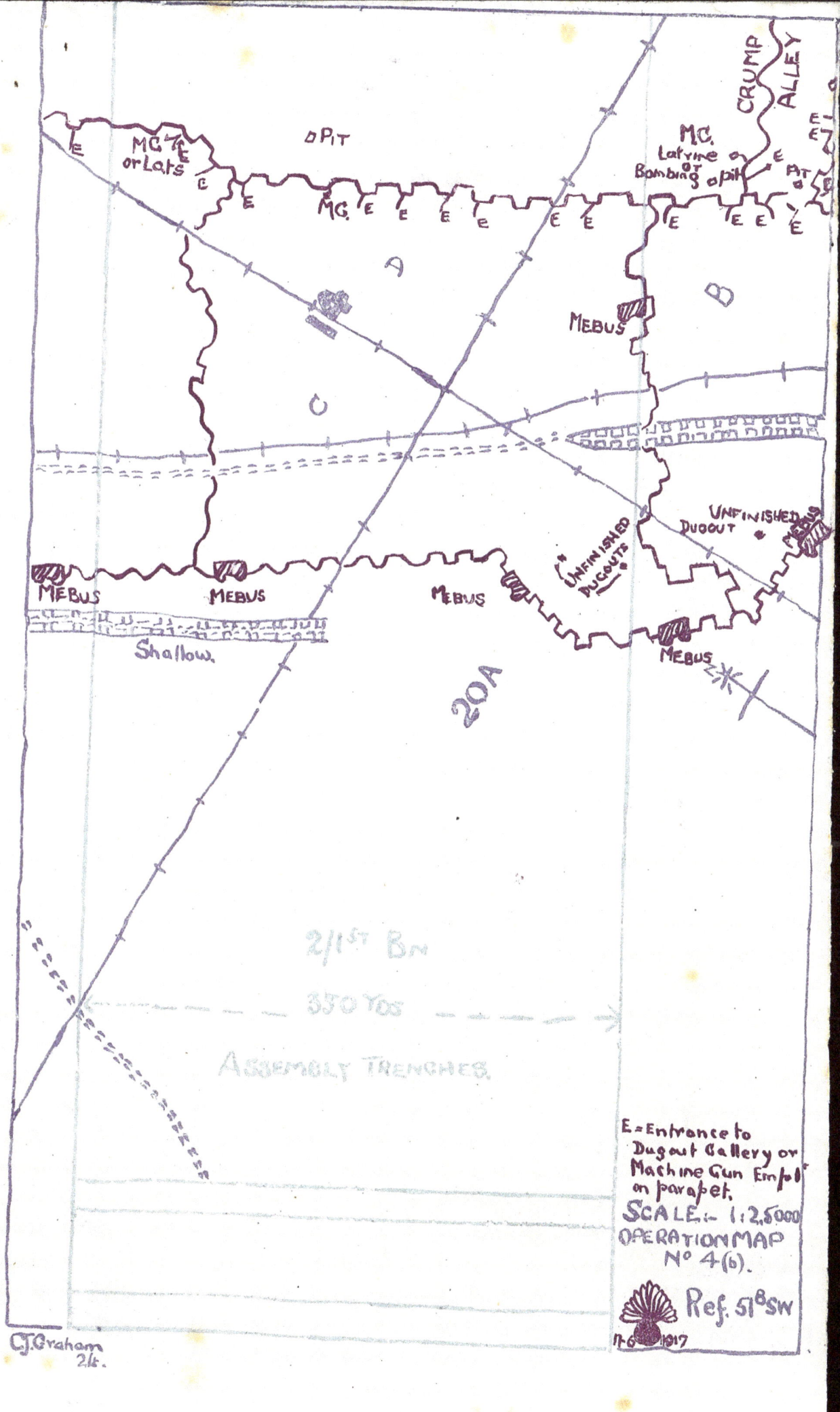

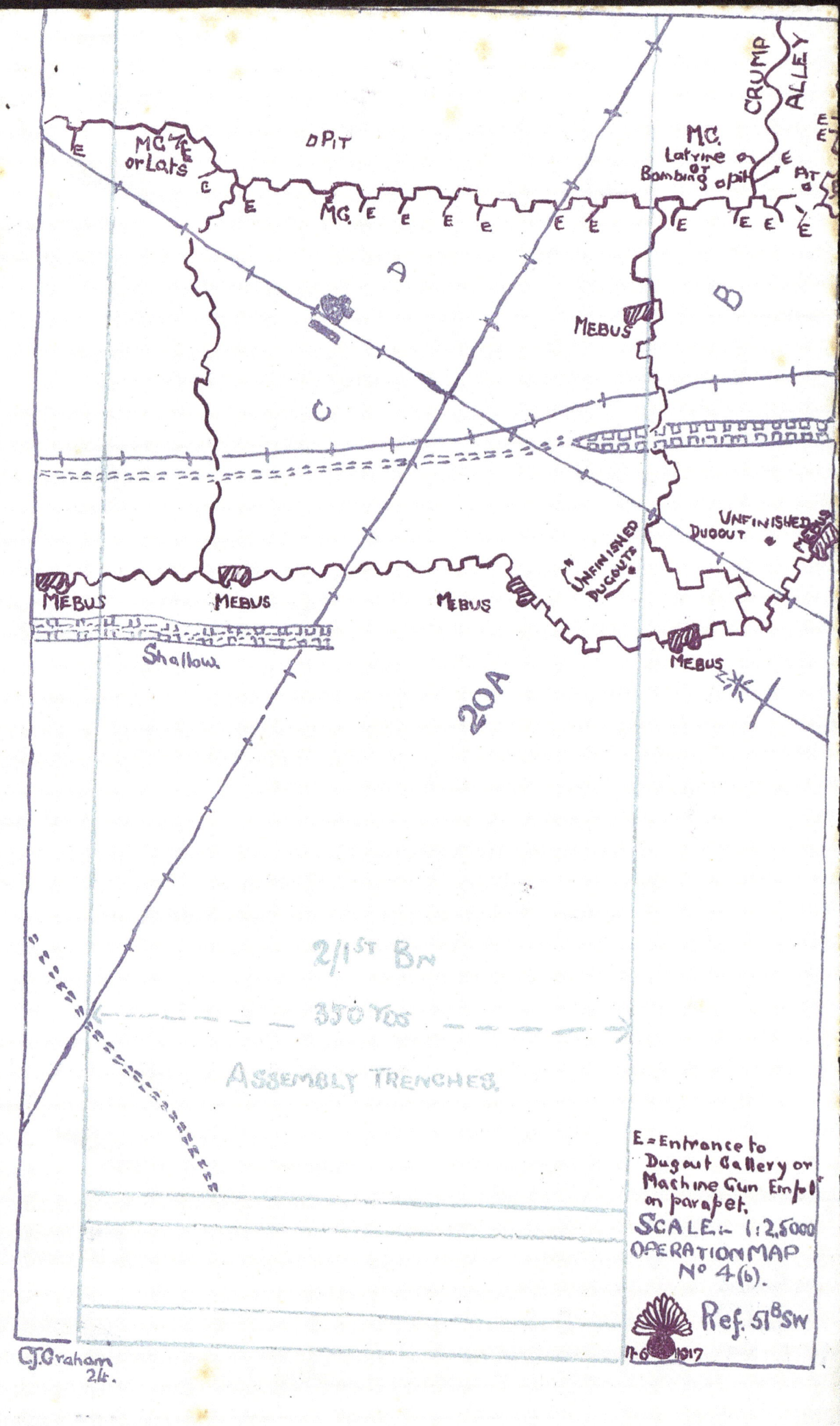

SCALE 1:2,500. Reference 51BSW. SQUARE "U". C.J.Graham.
OPERATION MAP No 4(a) 2/Lt.
E = Entrance to Dugout Gallery or M.G emplacement on parapet.

SCALE 1:2,500. Reference 51BSW. SQUARE "U".   C.J.Graham.
OPERATION MAP. Nº 4(a)   2/Lt.

E = Entrance to Dugout Gallery or M.G. emplacement on parapet.

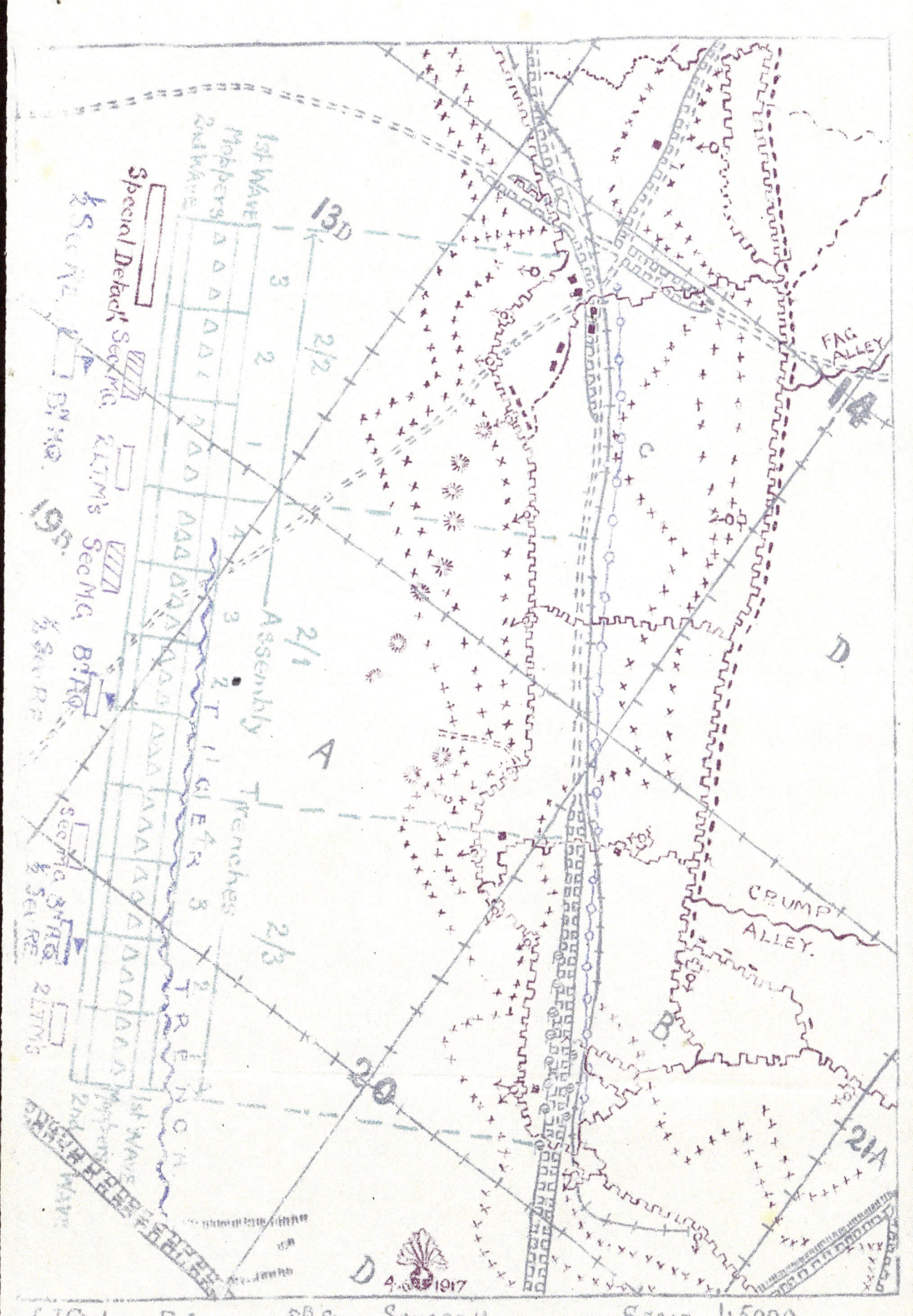

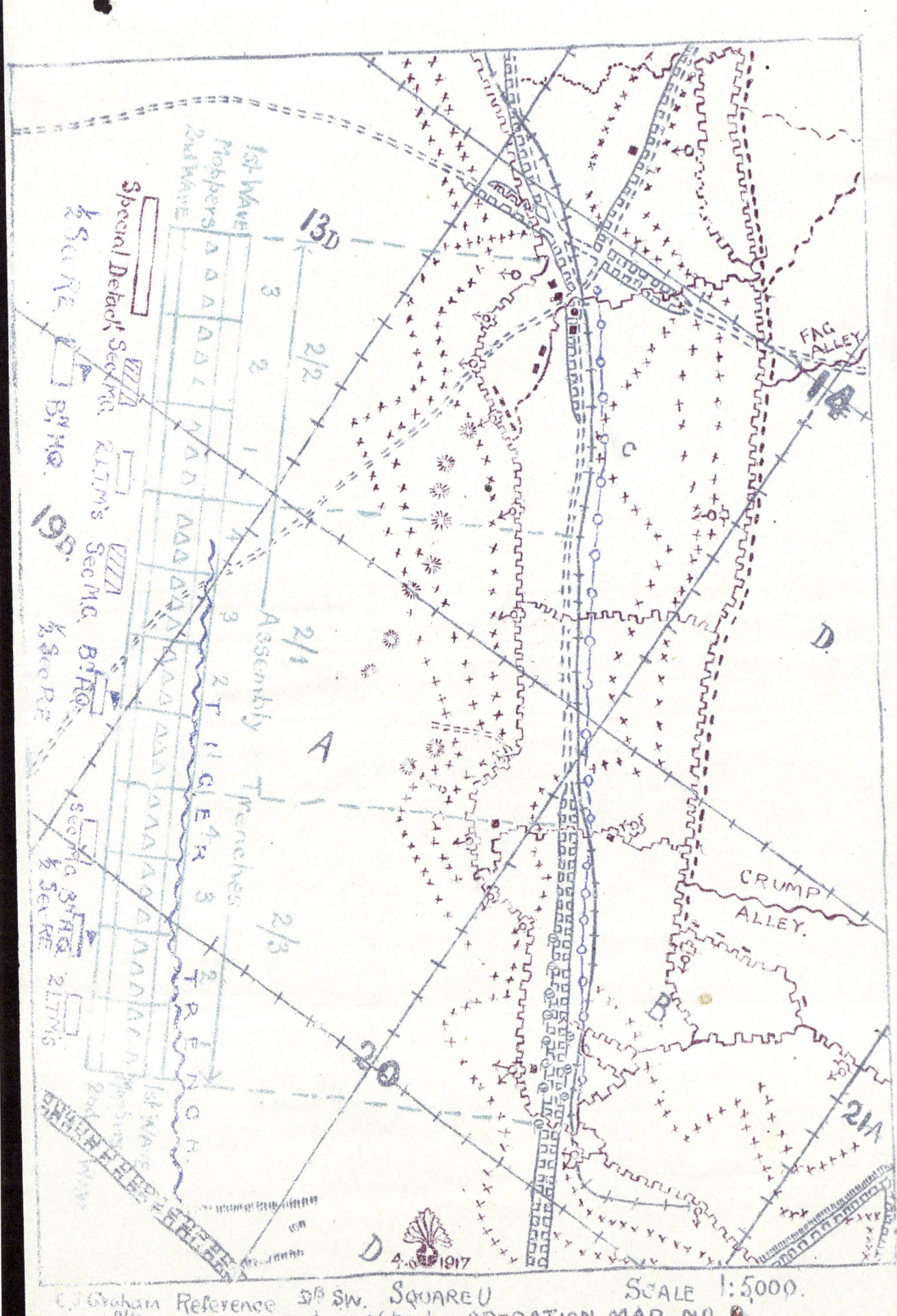

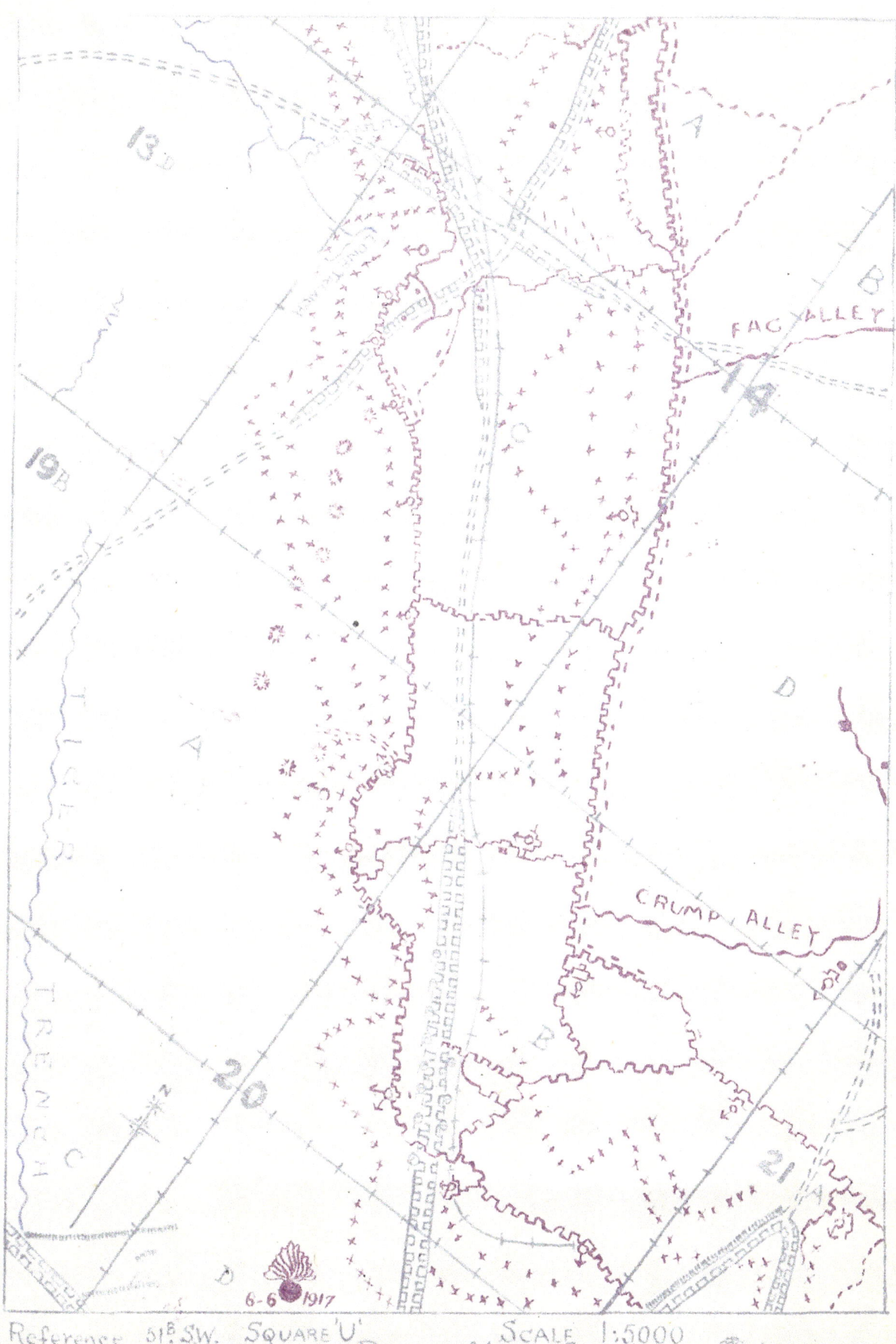

Reference 51.B S.W. Square 'U' Scale 1:5000
REPORT MAP No. 1

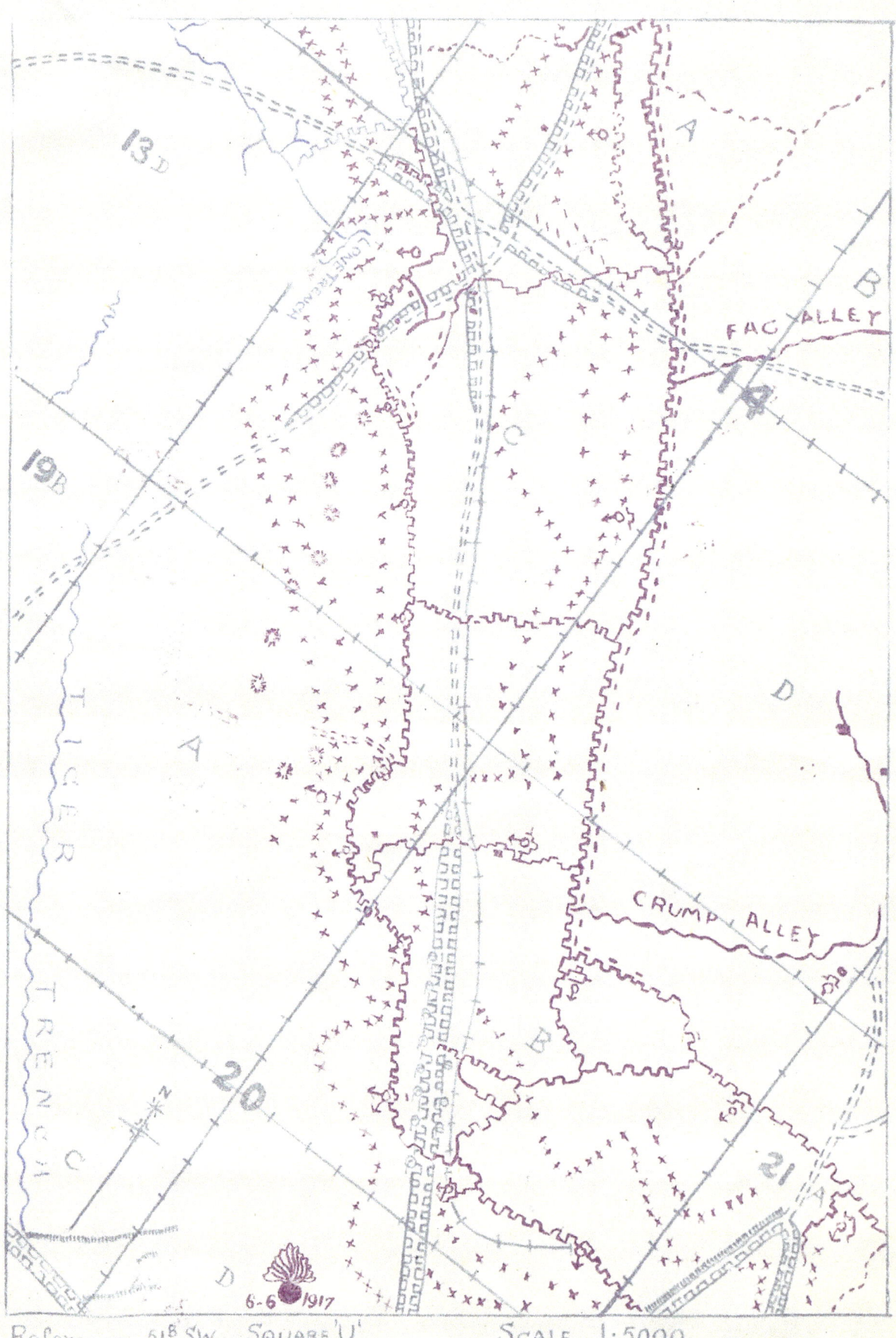

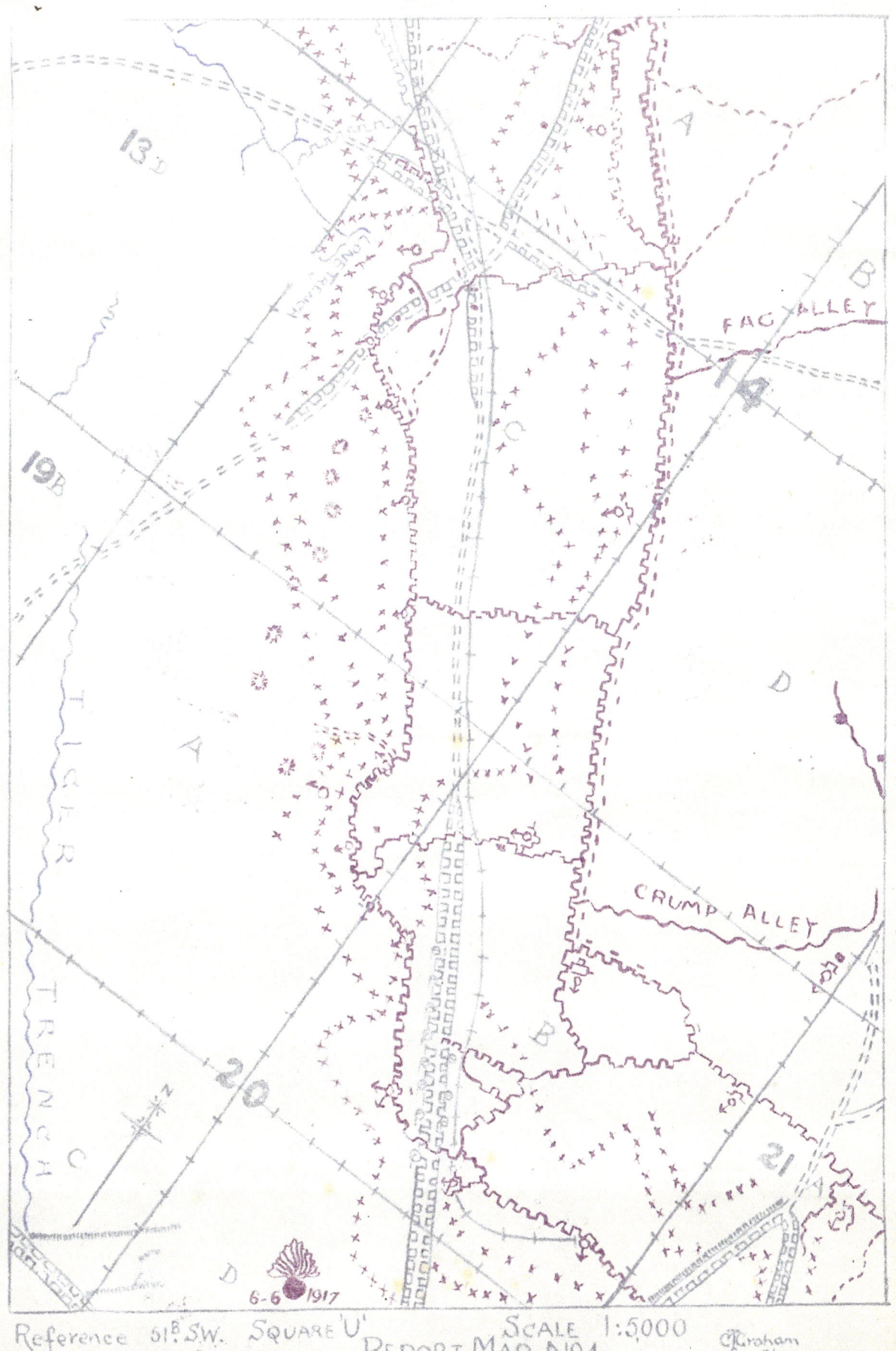

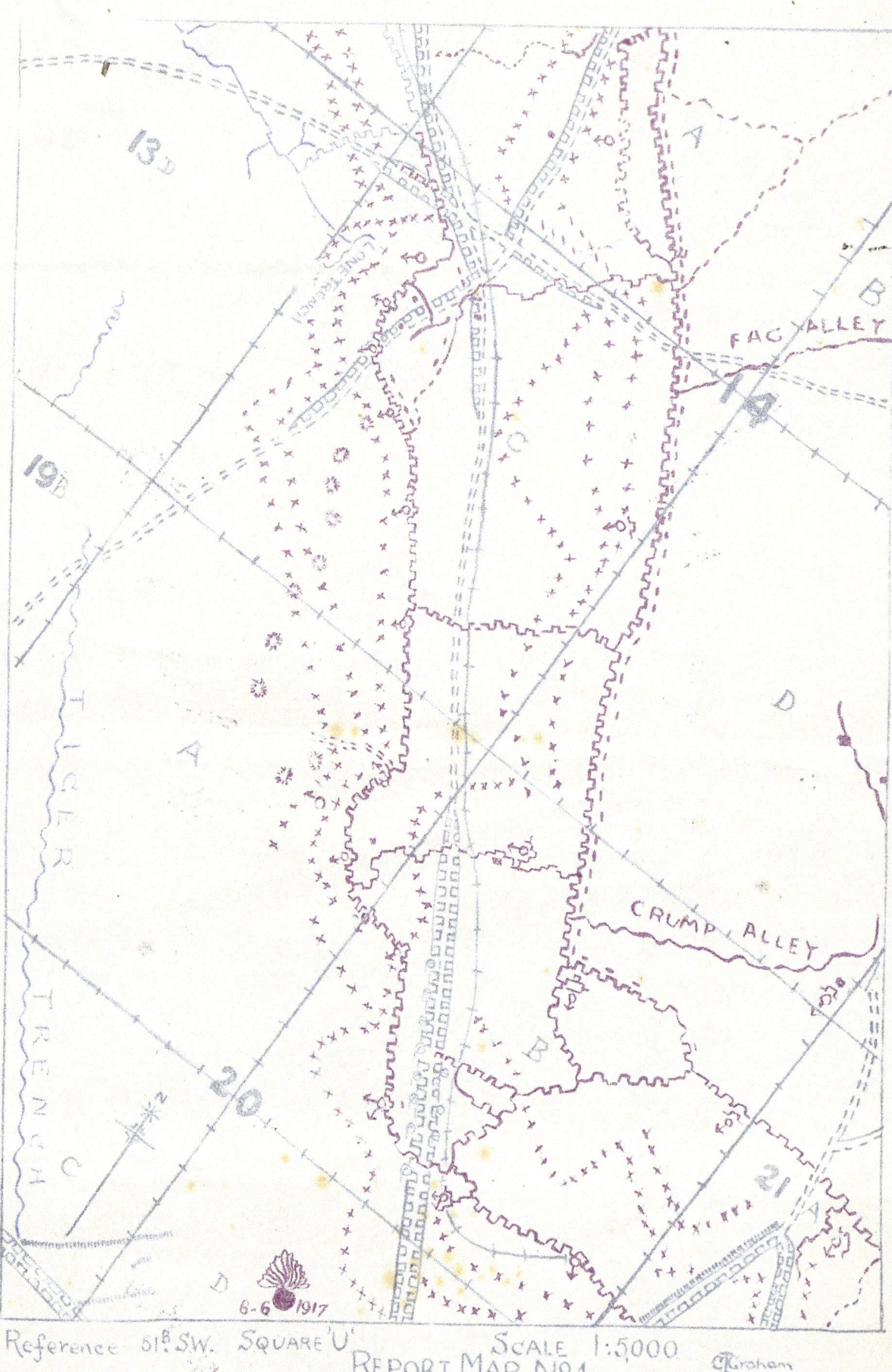

Reference 51.b S.W. Square 'U'   SCALE 1:5000
REPORT MAP No 1.

3. ASSEMBLY
   AREAS

   Units will move to their
   respectively assembly areas and well
   under allotted positions (see App A)
   by zero hour.

   The greatest care should be taken
   to avoid unnecessary movement and
   noise forward of the Railway Embankment
   All movement will be carefully screen
   as all are in view of the open.

   To avoid confusion, guide tapes will
   be laid from the line Embankment by
   Battalions concerned.

   The areas allotted to either
   of the Assembly areas will come under
   the command of O.C. Battalions
   concerned from 7 p.m. on Y day.

4. ADVANCED
   BRIGADE
   HEAD
   QUARTERS

   Will be established in the Sunken
   Road at T.21.c.29 by 5 p.m. on
   Y day.

   There will be a Brigade Report
   Centre at Brigade Hqrs. This Report
   Centre will be used and all liaison
   sent by all the Centre quickly if
   Battalions.

   Runners will proceed there at
   (a) O.I.C.
   (b) R.E.L.O. 2

5. TIME
   HOUR
   OF
   ATTACK

   The attack

for the exact hour of assault, is is of what importance that the Infantry should keep close up to the artillery barrage, and advance wherever it lifts.

6. ARTILLERY SUPPORT. The 1/5th Infantry Bde. will be supported by the artillery of three Divisions, viz: 7th, 51st & 62nd Divisions assisted by the R.F.C. & the Heavy Artillery of ...

7. SCHEME OF ATTACK. A Creeping Up Bn. will take over front line from our present left to U.13.d.6.3 on right from 1/6th Infantry Brigade on the Division to be assist later.
 1/4th Bn. will press up by bombing if necessary, with right of 1/5th Bn. as soon as 2nd Objective has been reached.
 The 2/7th Bn. on our right, will also keep up and occupy the line of the sunken road from U.21.c.3.6. right of 2/5 Bn. as soon as Objective has been captured.

8. SPECIAL DETACHMENT. The Company of the 1/5th Battalion will advance and capture enemy strong point at U.14.a.15.00 and the cross roads at U.14.c.35.55.

9. VICKERS MACHINE GUNS. The advance will be supported by the guns of the 201st, 190th and 2nd Brigade Machine Gun Cos and the guns of the 2nd Division.
 After the capture of the 1st Objective O.C. 206 M.G. Co. will arrange for 6 M.Gs to take up their position in captured German line.

10. LIGHT TRENCH MORTARS

The O.C. 173rd L.T.M. Battery arranged for four guns to move up the trench to hold on as soon as the 1st objective is captured and the hostile barrage has ceased. O.C. 173rd L.T.M. Battery will confer with O's C. of the 1/5th, 2/5th and 1st Battns. as to arrange employment.

11. ADVANCE OF BATTALION HEADQUARTERS

Battalion Headquarters will not advance until the objective has been captured. A procedure of Headquarters will follow behind units and select a place for Headquarters and send back to notify the Bn. Commander. Bn. Commander will immediately send back location of new Bn. H.Q. to Brigade.

12. AEROPLANE CO-OPERATION

Contact aeroplanes will be used at daylight before the positions gained by the Infantry, in accordance with the principles lately practised in this Brigade.

Flares will not be used. Infantry will be issued with yellow oil cloth. There will be waved whenever an aeroplane sounds its horn. Yellow handkerchiefs will never otherwise be exposed.

13. SYNCHRONISATION OF WATCHES

Officers i/c of Barrage Guns will report at Brigade H.Q. at 6 p.m. on Z day to synchronise watches. Watches will again be synchronised at

1 hour before ZERO is reached, Brigade transportation from Brigade Headquarters will meet Battalion Headquarters for that purpose.

14. **CARRYING PARTY**
Officer Commanding "B" Coy to detail a carrying party [illegible] strong and Eight Picked Members of [illegible] to be given [illegible] for [illegible] time.

15. **EQUIPMENT**
[illegible] for all to be in battle order and carry:–
   170 rounds S.A.A.
   4 sandbags
   2 Iron rations
   1 Box respirator + P.H.G. Helmet
   1 [illegible]
   Pick or shovel
   Full waterbottle
   Aeroplane Signals
[illegible] to be [illegible] per [illegible] and will also carry rifles.

16. **NOTES**
all Ranks to be [illegible] forward with the necessity of maintaining their [illegible] and [illegible] brought on to their attack objective. All the objects to be gained must be carefully studied beforehand. [illegible] notes [illegible] as possible and if you are lucky [illegible]
To this [illegible] to be [illegible] as to [illegible] Company Commanders to be given all the possible

(C) Men will be warned to be specially
    on their guard against retaining documents
    taken from prisoners or civilians.

(D) The word RETIRE does not exist
    in this Army, any order will be immediately
    killed.

17. MACHINE GUNS OF ——— will co-operate
    as follows:—
        (1) Indirect Fire
        (2) accompany Infantry to consolidate

    At least one Section will be kept
    along ——————— to act as Barrage Guns.

    These Guns will not move forward
    but continue to deliver Indirect Fire and
    a protective Barrage Fire which latter
    will become a S.O.S Concentration fire

    After capture of the S.O. objective our
    Section and two Lewis Guns will move
    forward to remain in consolidating
    captured position. They will move from
    position detailed for them to most suitable
    position to carry out their tasks.

    These Guns will be placed under the
    orders of the Battalion Commanders from
    time to time, and will ——— have the
    same G.O. officer of the Lewis Gun attached
    to be found in ——— with O/C
    both —————— advised of their respective
    methods.

The distribution of guns for action is as
Fand A. Guns under 2nd Lieut Whitehead
Capt C.H. / 2 Battalion on Left Section [?]

The remaining Guns Batteries of A section
of A.C. & O. Coys under 2nd Lieut T.R.H.
Roberts on the off Batteries on Right
Section etc.

Lieut Paterson will send C.A Coy
to the off bank to form an escort for the above
Section.

Guns (F)(C)(D) · (E) under 2nd Lieut R.H.
Roberts & 2nd Lieut N.R. Whitlock will be
detailed as Garrison Guns & will not move
forward.

Guns (F) & (H) & (B) under 2nd Lieut R.A.
Paterson & 2nd Lieut G.P. Butt will act
Garrison & also as Barrage Fire, but must be
prepared for move forward if the time to
release from detailed capacities.

The duties of these Barrage Guns will be
to deliver an overhead Barrage two from
stocked positions, they will be marked on Battr
by pole as detailed in Indirect Fire Chart &
map attached, and times as detailed in Fire
Chart also attached.

Preparation for Garrison Guns must
be made as soon as possible in accordance to
billeting instruction as if for night station

The Infantry Baggage will be maintained till situation is satisfactory, when it will cease to remain static and be spread at regular intervals, throughout the day and night. It will need to strafe fire in event of anything unusual.

AMMUNITION — at first made available by F.A. Ammunition will be dumped at Embankment under a NCO detailed by .... at keeper.

AMMUNITION / GENERAL DUMPS
FOR FORWARD & BARRAGE GUNS

FORWARD An Ammunition Dump will be
GUNS   established for forward guns at Tr. G.33
    a. Dug out ....

    These Dumps will be established by
    the forward guns concerned.

BELTS FOR   50 Belts in Belt Boxes per gun will
FORWARD GUNS   be supplied by forward guns during advance
    + spare belts per gun will be at Dump
    at Tr. K ... and will on no circumstances
    will ..... be touched by Barrage men.
    A NCO will be detailed in charge of this
    Dump by O.C. Barrage Guns.

BARRAGE   Dump for ..... Guns will be established
GUNS   in the vicinity of ....
    ..... Dump supplied ..... will be under
    ..... control in support of Barrage Guns.

BELTS FOR   ... belts filled at each Gun.
BARRAGE
GUNS

BELT FILLING
MACHINES

S O S

PROTECTIVE BARRAGE FIRE TABLE

GUN	TARGET	RANGE TO TARGET	CONTOUR YARDS GUN	CONTOUR YARDS TARGET	V I	Q E	EQUIV RANGE	CONTOUR OWN TROOPS	RANGE OWN TROOPS	ACTUAL CLEARANCE	
H	See Red Shading on Map	2200	77	100	23	359'	2300	96	1500	165'	
G	"	2300	77	100	23	393'	2400	100	1500	165'	
E	"	2200	92	96	4	328'	2200	100	1500	144'	
F	"	2200	92	96	4	328'	2200	100	1500	144'	
A	"	2000/2200	105	90	15	230'	1900	90	1500	——	does not fire over own troops
B	"	2100/2400	105	88	17	259'	2000	96	1400	198'	" "
10	"	2000	100	92	8	243'	2000	105	1300	147'	" "
8	"	2000	100	92	8	243'	2000	105	1300	147'	" "

Calculations made by J. F. Phillips Captain
O C 2nd Battery

AMENDED MACHINE GUN BARRAGE TIME TABLE

ZERO	BARRAGE OPENS ON TO TARGETS AS DETAILED IN INDIRECT FIRING CHART ALT. WITH AN EXTRA 100' OF ELEVATION
ZERO + 3	BARRAGE LIFTS 100'
ZERO + 6	" ANOTHER 100'
ZERO + 9	" ANOTHER 100'
ZERO + 12 UNTIL POSITION SATISFACTORY	DROPS TO S.O.S CONCENTRATION LINE AS PROTECTIVE BARRAGE

Confidential 58/bw1
Vol 4

May Deany
Job for C Hunt
from 21/5/11 to 31/6/11

WAR DIARY
of
26 M.G. Coy
1.1.17 to 31.1.17

WAR DIARY or INTELLIGENCE SUMMARY

Army Form C. 2118.

Vol I Page 18

Place	Date	Hour	Summary of Events and Information	Remarks and references to Appendices
ABLAINZEVELLE	1/7/1917		Programme of Work carried out. Working party of 2 officers + 50 O.R. found for Corps R.E. Dump at ACHIET-LE-GRAND	
Do	2/7/1917		Programme of Work carried out. Weather fine. One O.R. rejoined from Hospital.	
Do	3/7/1917		Programme of Work carried out	
Do	4/7/1917		Programme of Work carried out. Corps Commander awarded the Military Medal to No 16040 Sergt TANN.J.W. and No 28351 Corporal CONROY. W. Sergt TANN J.W. proceeded on ten days leave to U.K. with ration allowance.	
Do	5/7/1917		Programme of Work carried out.	
Do	6/7/1917		Programme of Work carried out. No 44134 Pte STEVENSON. H. proceeded on Special leave to U.K. for one month. Auth. G.H.Q. letter. A.G. D/1779/404 dated 3/7/17	
Do	7/7/1917		Programme of Work carried out. One O.R. admitted to Hospital.	
Do	8/7/1917		Company struck camp at ABLAINZEVELLE and proceeded by road via COURCELLES, SAPIGNIES and BAUPAUME to BANCOURT.	
BANCOURT	9/7/1917		Company proceeded by road to RUYAULCOURT via HAPLINCOURT, BERTINCOURT + took over Camp from 127 Machine Guns Co.	
RUYAULCOURT	10/7/1917		Programme of work carried out. One O.R. rejoined from Leave.	
"	11/7/17		Programme of work carried out. One man previously in not Camp. 2 O.R. admitted to Hospital	
"	/17		Programme of work carried out. One O.R. admitted to Hospital.	

WAR DIARY or INTELLIGENCE SUMMARY

Army Form C. 2118.

Place	Date	Hour	Summary of Events and Information	Remarks and references to Appendices
RUYAULCOURT	13/7/17		Programme of work carried out. One O.R. admitted to Hospital.	
"	14/7/17		Programme of work carried out. Company were inspected by Coys Commander.	
"	15/7/17		Programme of work carried out	
"	16/7/17		Programme of work carried out. One O.R. rejoined from leave. One O.R. admitted to Field Hospital.	
"	17/7/17		Company moved off in sections at intervals of 15 minutes to METZ. Company relieved No 198 R.E.Co. in the Line.	
METZ EN COUTURE	18/7/17		Front quiet. Infantry patrols were sent out during night. Casualties nil.	
"	19/7/17		Front quiet. Infantry reported that a large German patrol was out at 2.15 a.m. During the night usual bursts of M.G. fire from Enemy, usually the harassing. Some rifle grenades dropped on our wire. Work on a dug out for 2 man commenced. Our trenches did not fire. Casualties nil.	
"	20/7/17		Our Artillery were active on the left from 10.40 p.m. to 11.45 p.m. Enemy Artillery also active. Four enemy aeroplanes passed over our lines at a great height. Work done:- Emplacements improved, trench deepened & communication trench strengthened. Our Machine Guns did not fire. Casualties nil.	
"	21/7/17		From 10 p.m. to 11.30 p.m. Enemy bombarded our trenches, but no damage done to our gun positions. One of our guns caught a German working party, who had evidently lost their way. Result of the fire was not seen. Friendly working parties & patrols were sent out. Two of our guns fired in response to S.O.S call. Work done:- New M.G. Emplacement made & others improved. Casualties nil.	

WAR DIARY
or
INTELLIGENCE SUMMARY

(Erase heading not required.)

Army Form C. 2118.

Place	Date	Hour	Summary of Events and Information	Remarks and references to Appendices
METZ EN COUTURE	22/7/17		Front quiet. Work done:- Machine Gun emplacement, enforced. Our machine guns did not fire. Casualties nil.	
	23/7/17		Front quiet. Indirect Machine Gun fire on Sunken Road L.31.d; also on Enemy's front line, from 11 p.m. to 2 a.m. a total of 28500 rounds fired from 4 Guns. Further improvements made to Gun emplacements. Casualties nil. No 3 Section relieved No 4 Section.	
	24/7/17		The front quiet generally. Strong Infantry patrols & wiring parties were out all night. Two of our machine guns fired 8000 rounds between 11 p.m. & 3 a.m. on enemy roads L.32.c. 8.0.5. Enemy Machine Guns replied strongly to our fire of previous night. Casualties nil.	
	25/7/17		Our Infantry patrols & working parties out at intervals. Enemy sent over Gas shells on Ruby Alley. Enemy machine guns active; snipers were also active. Work done:- large dug out in front line almost completed. Casualties nil	
	26/7/17		Front quiet generally. Our machine guns did not fire. Work completed:- 2 Dug outs Ammunition Dump, Anti-aircraft position. Trenches around Gun positions cleaned and enforced. Casualties nil.	
	27/7/17		Front normal. Two of our M. Gunsfired, & enemy retaliated. Casualties nil.	
	28/7/17		Enemy Artillery very active. A raid was carried out by Infantry on our right. Three of our guns put down barrage fire in support. Casualties nil.	
	29/7/17		Front very quiet. Our Machine Guns did not fire. Casualties nil.	
	30/7/17		Front quiet. Some shelling by enemy artillery. Our Machine Guns did not fire.	

WAR DIARY
INTELLIGENCE SUMMARY

Army Form C. 2118.

21.

Place	Date	Hour	Summary of Events and Information	Remarks and references to Appendices
METZ EN COUTURE	31/7/17		Front quiet generally. Coy. H.Q. removed from Trety to NEUVILLE BOURTONVAL. Company relieved by 27 M.G. Coy. and took over Camp at NEUVILLE BOURTONVAL. Casualties nil. L.J.L. Price Captain O.C. No 206 M.G. Coy.	

Army Form C. 2118.

WAR DIARY
or
INTELLIGENCE SUMMARY.
(Erase heading not required.)

VOL I.
Page.

Instructions regarding War Diaries and Intelligence Summaries are contained in F. S. Regs., Part II. and the Staff Manual respectively. Title pages will be prepared in manuscript.

Place	Date	Hour	Summary of Events and Information	Remarks and references to Appendices
NEUVILLE	1/8/17		Company moved to MANIN by Bus accompanied by 10 officers & 66 O.R. of the 2/2nd and 2/4 London Regiment. Transport moved to ABLAINZEVELLE by road. Weather wet.	
MANIN	2/8/17		Company occupied day in clearing guns etc. Stores inspected. Transport of Company arrived. Weather wet.	
	3/8/17		Programme of work carried out. One O.R. granted leave to U.K. Weather showery.	
	4/8/17		Programme of work carried out. No 4 Section took over four anti-aircraft positions from the 4th Division - two guns at ROELLECOURT DUMPS at T.27a.26 and T.27 a.96, two guns at LIGNY ST FLOCHEL DUMP at T.23 d.18 and T.24 a.01. Weather unsettled.	
	5/8/17		Programme of work carried out. 2nd Lieut J Watkins joined Company from Base Depot. 2nd Lieut Rylance and 2 O.R. proceeded to Rest Camp. One O.R. admitted to Hospital.	
	6/8/17		Programme of Work carried out. 3 O.R's paraded with 2/3 Battalion London Regiment party for instruction in wiring, revetting, digging etc. under R.Es. Brigade Musketry officer inspected officers and N.C.O's with Revolvers near Range at I.18.b. Lieut H.01. Duffield proceeded to 175 M.G. Co to take over command. One O.R. granted leave to U.K. 2 other Ranks returned from Rest Camp. Weather fine.	
	7/8/17		Programme of work carried out, including night operations.	
	8/8/17		Programme of work carried out. - Digging of emplacements & revetting with sandbags.	
	9/8/17		Programme of work carried out. One O.R granted leave to U.K. One O.R. admitted to Hospital.	
	10/8/17		Programme of work carried out. A reinforcement of 3 O.R's reported this day.	
	11/8/17		Programme of Work carried out. Brigadier General inspected Company Transport.	
	12/8/17		Programme of Work carried out. No 3 Section relieved No 4 Section at ROELLECOURT and LIGNY ST FLOCHEL. One O.R admitted to Hospital.	
	13/8/17		Programme of Work carried out. One other Rank admitted to Hospital.	
	14/8/17		Programme of Work carried out.	
	15/8/17		Programme of Work carried out. One O.R. discharged from Hospital. One O.R. granted leave to U.K.	

WAR DIARY
INTELLIGENCE SUMMARY.

Army Form C. 2118.

Place	Date	Hour	Summary of Events and Information	Remarks and references to Appendices
MAROEUIL	16/8/17		Programme of work carried out. Weather fine	
"	17/8/17		BRIGADE SPORTS held at AMBRINES. Weather unsettled	
"	18/8/17		Programme of work carried out. Stormy	
"	19/8/17		Programme of work carried out. 2 O.R. proceeded to out Camp. Reinforcement of one O.R. reported this day.	
"	20/8/17		Programme of work carried out. Weather fine	
"	21/8/17		Programme of work carried out. One O.R. admitted to Hospital. Two O.R. discharged from Hospital.	
"	22/8/17		Programme of work carried out	
"	23/8/17		Programme of work carried out	
"	24/8/17		Company & Transport moved off to and entrained at AUBIGNY and detrained at POPERINGHE. Transport proceeded to DIRTY BUCKET CAMP A.30.C. Ref 28 Belgium France 1/40000	
"	25/8/17		Party of 108 O.R. under two officers disentrained Transport of 173 Infantry Brigade & No 2 Signal Co. Party arrived at DIRTY BUCKET CAMP at 6 p.m.	
"	26/8/17		Company moved to RIEGERSBURG CAMP. 4 Sections of 4 guns each, moved up to the line to await 48th Division. Guns were moved as follows:- 1 and 2 Sections as "B" Battery, located at C.11.C.95 (ALBERTA) and 3 & 4 Sections as "C" Battery located at C.11.C. 30.95 (ALBERTA) MAP REF POELCAPELLE 1/10000. 64 O.R. of 2/1 London Regt. attached Coy as Carriers.	
"	27/8/17		Zero hour for attack 1.55 p.m. Fire maintained according to Barrage Time Table attacked. Casualties nil. Weather wet, causing frequent stoppages to gun swing & mud. all guns fired well under these conditions. following prolonged stoppages occurred:- 2 Broken fuzee springs; 2 bulged barrels. 140000 rounds of ammunition were fired. Enemy Barrage fell on the line of Steenbeek about 400 yards in front of our gun positions. Enemy Barrage was fairly heavy, and lasted 6½ hours.	

WAR DIARY
INTELLIGENCE SUMMARY.
(Erase heading not required.)

Army Form C. 2118.

Place	Date	Hour	Summary of Events and Information	Remarks and references to Appendices
	28/8/17		Weather wet. Enemy artillery quiet during day. Company relieved 4 Guns of the 144th M.G. Coy on the night of the 28/29th and 4 Guns of the 143rd M.G. Co. 2 Guns of No.1. Section took over positions at SPRINGFIELD. Relief complete by 3 a.m. Casualties one O.R. wounded. 4 Guns of No 2. Section took over positions MONDUHIBU and TRIANGLE FARM. Relief complete by 3 a.m. Casualties Nil. 1. Gun No 4 Section took over position at C.12 D.83. Relief complete by 3.30 a.m. Casualties Nil. 4 Guns of No 3 Section took up positions on the line ALBERTA - REGINA CROSS. 5. Guns maintained in Reserve at ALBERTA. (Company H.Q.) B4 POELLECAPELLE 1/10,000	
	29/8/17		Enemy Artillery quiet. Our machine Guns did not fire. Weather wet cost 195th M.G. Co. relieved the guns in MONDUHIBU and TRIANGLE FARM, and on the ALBERTA - REGINA CROSS Line. Relief complete by 12 midnight. Casualties 2nd 215th M.G. Co. relieved Guns at SPRINGFIELD and the Gun at C.12. D.83. Relief complete by 5 a.m. Casualties Nil. All Transport was unable to get beyond BOUNDARY ROAD owing to Enemy shelling.	
	30/8/17		Company with Transport moved to DAMBRE CAMP 28 N.W. 1/20000. POELLCAPELLE	
	31/8/17		Reorganisation and generally cleaning up. Weather showery	

Barrage Time Table

Battery	Location	Firing From Zero +	Firing To Zero +	Target	Rate of Fire
B	Alberta	0	25		3000 rounds per hour decreasing
		25	3:30	D7.6.25.10 to D1.6.85.10	to 1000 per hour at Zero plus 3
		3:30	4:30	D8.a.40.70 to D1.d.83.60	increasing to 3000 at Zero + 66
		5.5	5:25	D2.c.15.50 to D1.6.90.45	and continuing to Zero plus 98,
				ditto	then decreasing to 1000 till Zero plus 4:30 cease fire.
					To open at Zero plus 5.5 at 3000 and continue until Zero plus 5:25 cease fire
C	Alberta	0	25	D1.d.30.25 - D1.a.90.20	
		25	3:30	D1.d.85.60 - D1.b.30.50	On S.O.S open at 6000 per hour
		3:30	4:30	D1.6.90.35 - V.25.d.4.4	for 10 minutes decrease to 3000 at 20 minutes then 1000 for
		5.5	5:25	ditto	30 minutes.

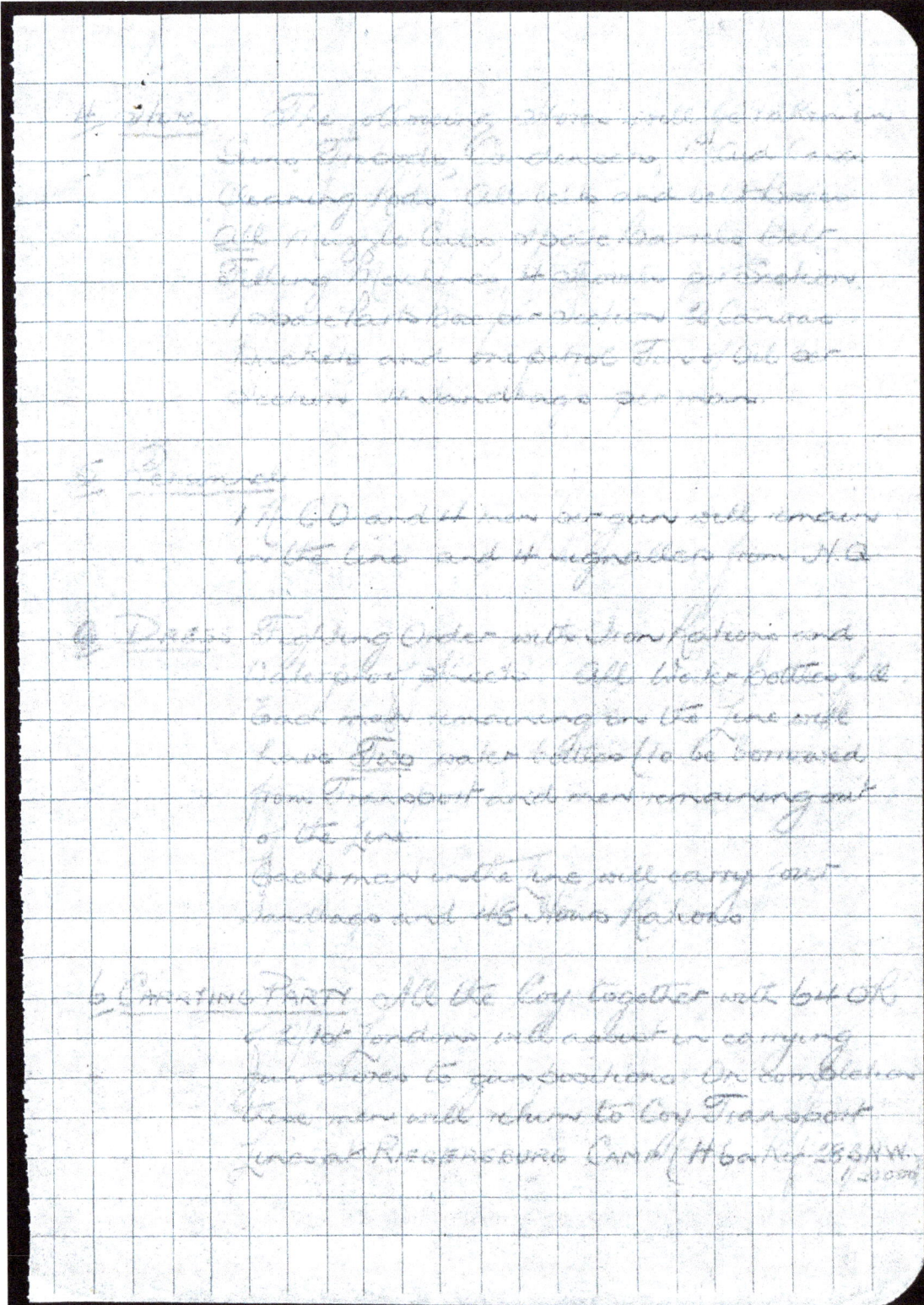

7. <u>Work</u>   All work on gun positions will be
            completed on Y/Z night

8. <u>TRANSPORT</u>   2 limbers per Section will be used
            to carry gun stores detailed in Para 4
            Pack saddlery will be placed on limbers
            on arrival at advanced dump
                O.C. Bell will be responsible that
                    1 mile double wire
                    2 Buggers
            are placed in one of the limbers and
            unloaded at ALBERTA

9. Coy HQ   at ALBERTA
            Rear HQ   at REIGERSBURG Camp

10. <u>Watches</u> will be synchronised on Zero day

11. A Belt Filling depôt will be established near
    the gun positions exact position will be notified
                                                    later

12. All section officers will render their Indirect Fire
    Charts to Orderly Room by 10.30 am

13. **Move** The Coy with Transport, will parade ready to move from this Camp at 12.30pm tomorrow on the pen given by the Transport Lines. Picks will be dumped on arrival at the New Camp (REIGERSBURG CAMP) H.6 on Ref 2/RNW 1/2.

14. Administrative Orders are issued separately

Copy No 1 to Seer of Coys
  2 O.m. Co/H8 Bn
  3 173rd Bde. H.Q.
  4 War Diary

Army Form C. 2118.

WAR DIARY
INTELLIGENCE SUMMARY.
(Erase heading not required.)

VOL 1

Instructions regarding War Diaries and Intelligence Summaries are contained in F.S. Regs., Part II. and the Staff Manual respectively. Title pages will be prepared in manuscript.

206 M.G. COY

Place	Date	Hour	Summary of Events and Information	Remarks and references to Appendices
DAMBRE CAMP	Sept 1/9/17		Programme of Work carried out. Enemy aircraft appeared over Camp. Our machine guns fired 19 rounds at them.	
"	2/9/17		Programme of Work carried out. Our Machine Guns fired 260 rounds at Enemy aeroplanes.	
"	3/9/17		Programme of Work carried out. 40 rounds fired at Enemy planes.	
"	4/9/17		Programme of Work carried out. Enemy appeared in vicinity of Camp. Our machine guns fired 30 rounds at them.	
"	5/9/17		Programme of Work carried out. 2nd Lieut H.R. Walbeck admitted to Hospital this day.	
"	6/9/17		Programme of Work carried out.	
"	7/9/17		Programme of Work carried out. 3 Other Ranks reported this day.	
"	8/9/17		Programme of Work carried out.	
"	9/9/17		Programme of Work carried out. 1 Other Rank admitted to Hospital.	
"	10/9/17		Programme of Work carried out. 2nd Lieut W.G. Scott transferred to 214 Machine Gun Co.	
"	11/9/17		Company moved to Regimental Camp in afternoon. At night Company relieved 8 Guns of 198 Machine Gun Co in Left Sector and 8 Guns of 215 Machine Gun Co in Right Sector N.W. YPRES. Casualties Nil.	

WAR DIARY / INTELLIGENCE SUMMARY

Army Form C. 2118.

Place	Date	Hour	Summary of Events and Information	Remarks and references to Appendices
	12/9/17		Enemy Artillery active between hours 1 a.m. and 4 a.m.; 11.30 a.m. and 12.30 p.m. and 4 p.m. to 5 p.m., a quantity of Gas shells mixed with H.E. were sent over at intervals. Work done – Improving positions and pumps & water out of emplacements. Our Machine Guns fired 2000 rounds on Enemy roads during day. Casualties – Pte. No 3 Section were relieved by 4 Guns of 2/14 Bn B. Coy and moved into reserve at REIGERSBURG CAMP.	
	13/9/17		Hostile Artillery normal. Enemy M. Gun active. Position taken up to be located for retaliation. Our machine Guns did not fire. Work on improving emplacements continued. Casualties nil.	
	14/9/17		at 3 a.m. our artillery put down barrage along the front – 3 minutes after enemy barrage commenced. Barrage lasted an hour and half, and consisted mostly of 4.25 and 5.9s. Enemy machine guns throughout night active. Work done :– Dug outs cleaned. Casualties 1 O.R. Killed and 1 O.R. wounded. Our Machine Guns fired continuously on WINNIPEG FARM, Ref map POELCAPELLE 1/10000.	
	15/9/17		Hostile Artillery moderately active. Enemy searched for batteries in rear of our gun with gas and H.E. shells. About 6.15 p.m. and again at 7.15 p.m. a dense white cloud appeared on our front, – about 1000 yards east of SPRINGFIELD – evidently a discharge of gas. It dispersed before reaching our positions but was distinctly smelt. Work done – Improving dugouts etc. Casualties nil. Our Machine Guns fired 2000 rounds on enemy tracks.	

WAR DIARY
INTELLIGENCE SUMMARY.
(Erase heading not required.)

Army Form C. 2118.

Place	Date	Hour	Summary of Events and Information	Remarks and references to Appendices
	16/9/17		Enemy Artillery very active. Hostile Machine Guns fired on our positions at intervals during night. Casualties Nil.	
	17/9/17		Artillery very active on both sides. Enemy sent over quantity of gas and H.E. shells. Our Machine Guns fired on tracks during night. Work done:- Improving dugouts & pumping out water. Casualties Nil.	
	18/9/17		Nos 2 and 3 sections moved up into CANOPUS TRENCH on 6.1.S.3.O. Ref Map POELCAPELLE 1/10000. Work done. - Eight Machine Gun Emplacements were constructed in this trench and eight more at TEST HILL. at 1.30.pm our Artillery put down barrage on Enemy positions. Our Machines did not fire owing to Ranks wounded. Enemy shell fell near Transport Lines at DAMBRE CAMP killing 2 mules and wounding 2 others. One mule destroyed owing to injuries received whilst taking up ammunition to Battery Dump.	
	19/9/17		Enemy activity normal. Our Artillery fairly active. Our eight guns formerly T. Battery in CANOPUS TRENCH completed arrangements for Barrage work. No firing was carried out. Casualties Nil.	

Army Form C. 2118.

WAR DIARY
or
INTELLIGENCE SUMMARY.
(Erase heading not required.)

Instructions regarding War Diaries and Intelligence Summaries are contained in F.S. Regs., Part II. and the Staff Manual respectively. Title pages will be prepared in manuscript.

Place	Date	Hour	Summary of Events and Information	Remarks and references to Appendices
	20/9/17	5.40 a.m ZERO HOUR	Our machine guns No.1. Barrage opened from CANOPUS TRENCH, Battery V on to target given (23) and continued until 6.40. a.m. with intense fire. Rounds expended 34000 infront of our lines at SPRINGFIELD and two in vicinity of JANET FARM were mounted for the purpose of engaging (1) hostile aircraft (2) repelling counter attacks.	
		6 a.m	Four guns went forward and occupied following positions - One Gun to Shell hole D7.a.35.5.0, One Gun to Shell hole D7.a.05.1.0, One Gun to MEBUS C 12 d 6.5.8.0.; and one Gun to shell hole in area WINNIPEG Cross Roads. Ref. POELCAPELLE Map. 1/10000." All guns reached objectives with following casualties en route - 2 killed 3 wounded	
		6.40 a.m.	Battery V (8 guns) moved up in Artillery formation from CANOPUS TRENCH to JEW HILL through fairly heavy shelling without loss.	
		11.25 a.m.	The two gun teams in shell holes D7.a.05.5.0 and D7.a.05.1.0. reported knocked out. One officer, 2 guns and teams withdrawn from Battery V and ordered to go forward to occupy these positions.	
		14.10	Order received from Division to adopt our VI Target, and fire was opened at 15.50. Order received from Division to attack Target W.1 (214 M.G.Co.) (Target) and intense fire opened. Order also received for counter attack guns to barrage x 2 Target (214 M.G. Co. target), & order complied with.	
		15.40		
		15.55	Night was exceptionally quiet. Barrage Guns were dug in and emplacements connected up by spaced. Dug outs for teams and belt filling depot finished. Total Casualties for the day were 3. O.R. killed and 7. O.R. wounded.	

Army Form C. 2118.

WAR DIARY
or
INTELLIGENCE SUMMARY.

(Erase heading not required.)

Instructions regarding War Diaries and Intelligence Summaries are contained in F. S. Regs., Part II. and the Staff Manual respectively. Title pages will be prepared in manuscript.

Place	Date	Hour	Summary of Events and Information	Remarks and references to Appendices
	21/9/17		Company with the exception of No 3 Section were relieved by 215t Machine Gun Company and moved into DAMBRE CAMP. No. 3. Section took up positions in CANOPUS TRENCH. Enemy counter attack during day were repulsed our Machine Guns fired on their S.O.S. Targets. Casualties 3 other Ranks killed and 5 other Ranks wounded	
DAMBRE CAMP.	22/9/17		Company resting & cleaning Guns stores etc	
	23/9/17 24/9/17		No 3 Section engaged Hostile Aircraft from CANOPUS TRENCH, with Machine Gun fire at intervals. Casualties Nil	
	25/9/17		A reinforcement of 40 other Ranks reported this day. Nos 1 and 2 Sections forming Battery of 8 Guns, moved into position C.12.d.8.5.5.0. (approx) Bay Ref POELCAPPELLE 1/10000 and constructed emplacements and ammunition Casualties Nil	
	26/9/17		The Battery opened fire prompt at zero and carried on in accordance with instructions. Information being received that Germans were moving in KORSK 15 minutes interval fire was delivered on this place, followed by bursts at intervals at 16.50 upon orders being received from Divisional Battery, was ordered to "change" DUMP HOUSE TO KOREK by lifts of one minute each up and down. Rapid fire for 20 minutes was concentrated on this area, and afterwards by community fire Rounds expended during day 70000 (approx) Casualties 1 O.R wounded	
BRAKE CAMP	27/9/17		Company evacuated positions in the Line and returned to BRAKE CAMP by Light Railway. Casualties Nil	
"	28/29/9/17		Company resting. Transport went forward to new area. Hostile aircraft very active at night over the Camp. Casualties Nil	
	30/9/17		Company left BRAKE CAMP for PESELHOEK STATION to entrain for new area	

A5834 Wt.W4973/M687 750,000 8/16 D. D. & L. Ltd. Forms/C.2118/13.

Army Form W. 3121.

173rd Infantry Brigade. 55th Division. XVIII Corps. Date of Recommendation. Sept 23rd 1917

Regtl. No.	Rank and Name (Christian names must be stated)	Action for which commended (Date and place of action must be stated)	Recommended by	Honour or Reward	(To be left blank)
33507	Sergeant THOMAS YARE	20th/21st Sept 1917. N.W. YPRES. Under most trying conditions, he was invaluable to his officer, and his cheerful example inspired the necessary confidence in all his men to keep their guns going over a period of 48 hours, during which the gun positions were continuously shelled.		Military Medal	

Unit: 206 MACHINE GUN Co. transferred from 8TH LIVERPOOL IRISH

Army Form W. 3121.

Schedule No. (to be left blank)	Unit	Regtl. No.	Rank and Name (Christian names must be stated)	Action for which commended (Date and place of action must be stated)	Recommended by	Honour or Reward	(To be left blank)
173rd Brigade. 58th Division. XVIII Corps. Date of Recommendation. 23/9/17							
	206 M.G. Company transferred from 6th King's Own Yorkshire Light Infantry	20052	Corporal JOHN MARRIOTT	20/9/17 N.W. OF YPRES. He exercised the greatest skill in advancing with two Machine Gun and teams through a heavy barrage. By his judgment and leadership he reached his objective without casualties. He immediately consolidated and kept his guns firing even though the enemy's barrage was right on his gun positions		D.C.M.	

Army Form W. 3121.

173rd Infantry Brigade.		58 London Division.	XVIII Corps.	28th Sept 1917 Date of Recommendation.	
Schedule No. (to be left blank)	Unit	Regtl. No.	Rank and Name (Christian names must be stated)	Action for which commended (Date and place of action must be stated)	Recommended by	Honour or Reward	(To be left blank)

| | 206 Machine Gun Co. (1st B Battery M.G.C.) | | T/2e Lieut | OSMOND PHILIP PRATT. | This officer displayed gallantry and coolness in the handling of three machine gun teams during the operations at Bullecourt 15/6/17 to 17/6/17 and by his example inspired all ranks. This officer has in addition performed consistent good service for the period under review. | L. L. Pinckney Capt. OC 206 M.G.C. | Mentioned in Despatches |

Army Form W. 3121.

Schedule No.							
73rd Infantry Brigade.		58th Division.	XVIII Corps.	25th Sept 1917 Date of Recommendation.			
	Unit	Regtl. No.	Rank and Name (Christian names must be stated)	Action for which commended (Date and place of action must be stated)	Recommended by	Honour or Reward	(To be left blank)
	206 Machine Gun Co. and Regiment Royal Welsh Fusiliers	15102	Sergt. HARRISON DUNCAN.	This N.C.O. has performed exceptionally good work in conveying rations to the front line troops throughout the following engagements under heavy shell fire viz:- First Battle of Bullecourt 12/19 May 1917 Second Battle of Bullecourt 15 June 1917 Recent operations on this front 20/21 Sept 1917. On each of these occasions, due to the coolness and skill of this N.C.O. rations, stores, ammunition etc were delivered to places detailed with a minimum of loss and delay. In addition he has performed his duties as Transport Sergeant in a most satisfactory manner.	[signatures] O.C. 206 M.G.C.	Military Medal	[initials]

Army Form W. 3121.

Schedule No. (to be left blank)	Unit	Regtl. No.	Bank and Name (Christian names must be stated)	Action for which commended (Date and place of action must be stated)	Recommended by	Honour or Reward	(To be left blank)
	206 Machine Gun Co.		T/Sec. Lieut Arthur Ernest WAY	20/21st Sept 1917. N.W. of YPRES This officer displayed great coolness and skill in the handling of his machine guns under heavy fire. The positions he occupied were trenched for the consolidation of the captured ground, but were made untenable by shell fire. He reconnoitred the ground and chose new positions under trying conditions, and was able to save his two guns without endangering the scheme of defence. He has in addition performed his duties as Section Officer in a most satisfactory manner during the recent operations on unseen review.	[signature] Capt.	Mention in the Despatches	

173rd Infantry Brigade. 55th London Division. XVIII Corps. 25th Sept 1917 Date of Recommendation.

Army Form W. 3121.

173rd Infantry Brigade. **58th London** Division. **XVIII** Corps. Date of Recommendation **25th Sept 1917**

Schedule No. (to be left blank)	Unit	Regtl. No.	Rank and Name (Christian names must be stated)	Action for which commended (Date and place of action must be stated)	Recommended by	Honour or Reward	(To be left blank)
	206 Machine Gun Co. late Regt 1/10th London Regiment	445539	C.S.M. ERNEST ARTHUR WIGMORE	This Warrant Officer has shown skill and tact in the training and handling of N.C.O.'s and men of the Company. He has performed good service in and out of the line during the past six months. For exceptional coolness and skill in the handling of return parties at the First Battle of Bullecourt 12/19th May 1917 he was recommended for the Military Medal.	L J L Price Cpn [?] o/c 206 M.G.C.	C.M. Mention in Dispatches	

Army Form W. 3121.

Schedule No. (to be left blank)	Brigade.	Unit	Regtl. No.	Rank and Name (Christian names must be stated)	Division.	Corps.	Action for which commended (Date and place of action must be stated)	Recommended by	Date of Recommendation.	Honour or Reward	(To be left blank)
	173rd (6th)	206 M.G. Company. transferred from 103rd MG Training Reserve Bttn.	66044	Private FREDERICK EDWARDS	58th	XVIII	20th & 21st Sept. 1917. N.W. of YPRES. For exceptional bravery in the delivery of important dispatches. On all occasions he had to pass through the enemy barrage. His cool confidence was entirely responsible for the good cooperation of the Barrage Guns and enabled them to switch on to enemy concentrations in the shortest possible time. In addition he carried messages to the forward guns, the location of which was uncertain, and brought back most valuable information		23/9/17	D.C.M.	

Army Form W. 3121.

| Brigade. | ___ Infantry | Division. ___ | Corps. XVIII | Date of Recommendation. Sept 25 1917 |

Schedule No. (to be left blank)	Regtl. No.	Rank and Name (Christian names must be stated)	Unit	Action for which commended (Date and place of action must be stated)	Recommended by	Honour or Reward	(To be left blank)
	T/SEC LIEUT	REGINALD WALTER KEMP	206 Machine Gun Co	20th & 21st Sept 1917. N.W. of YPRES. Was in charge of a batter of machine guns and had to advance through a heavy enemy barrage in order to carry a his targets. By his skill and judgment he accomplished this without casualties. His gun positions were nearly shelled but his coolness and example inspired all his men to keep their guns firing. He carried out reconnaissance of difficult ground under harassing conditions, during his jump from target to target to exploit hostile concentrations. It was largely due to the grasping of situation so quickly that the enemy's counter attacks were disorganised before they materialised.		M C	

Army Form W. 3121.

Schedule No. (to be left blank)	Unit	Regtl. No.	Rank and Name (Christian names must be stated)	Action for which commended (Date and place of action must be stated)	Recommended by	Honour or Reward	(To be left blank)
	3rd Royal West Kent Regiment attached Machine Gun Corps 206 Company		Lieutenant LIONEL ERNEST HOWARD WHITBY	17/9/1917 N.W. of YPRES. For an extremely valuable reconnaissance of a forward position for 40 Machine Guns engaged in a Barrage. This reconnaissance was carried out under the most adverse conditions, in addition to the difficult nature of the ground, the area was swept by machine gun, rifle, and shell fire.	2 Lt R.M.C. Capt a/c 26 M.G.C.	M.C.	

173rd Inf Brigade. 58th Division. XVIII Corps. 23/9/17 Date of Recommendation.

206 MACHINE GUN Co. Copy No 2
OPERATION ORDER No 11

The 206 Machine Gun Company will relieve 198 Machine Gun Company and 215 Machine Gun Company on night of 11th/12th September 1917.

1. DISPOSITION

   Left Sector occupied by 8 guns of 198 Coy
   Right Sector occupied by 8 guns of 215 Coy.

   Disposition of guns in accordance with sketch map attached.

   Gun positions marked 1, 2, 3, 4 on Left Sector will be taken over by No. 3 Section.

   Gun positions marked 5, 6, 7, 8 on Left Sector will be taken over by No. 2 Section.

   Gun positions marked 9, 10, 11, 12 on Right Sector will be taken over by No. 4 Section.

   Gun positions marked 13, 14, 15, 16 on Right Sector will be taken over by No. 1 Section.

2. STORES ETC.

   Tripods, Belt Boxes will be handed over by outgoing teams, and gun commanders will see that everything is handed over in a thorough manner.

3. ADVANCE PARTY

   Lieut L. C. H. Whitby will remain for duty with Advanced Coy H.Q., which will be along Canal Bank (215 M.G. Coy H.Q). He will move to Coy H.Q with small advanced party, arriving there about 2.30 p.m to take over Billets etc. He will ascertain from Area Commandant any local rules.

1.

4. TRANSPORT AND Q.M STORES

Transport & Q.M Stores will be at DAMBRE CAMP. Attention of Transport Officer is directed to XVIII Corps Routine Order No 450 dated 6/9/17.

5. RATIONS.

Sections going into Line will take 2 day rations.

Ration Dump for Left Sector, Admirals Road Party of 6 from Rear H.Q will carry rations for the 2 Sections to Section H.Q at Bunt, e.g gun positions 7 and 8. From here, Rations for Section in front Line will be taken by a ration party from that Section at a prearranged time.

Ration Dump for Section in Right Sector will be on St JULIEN R⁰ C.18.a 1.5 9.5 From here, Ration parties will be found from Sections concerned.

6. WATER

Sections will take 2 days water supply. The Coy will draw 40 tins from Brigade H.Q These tins will be Trench Stores in this Brigade.

7. REFILLING POINT.

Water refilling point VLAMERTINGHE Cross Roads H.3.c.7.5.

8. GUIDES FOR LEFT SECTOR

Will be at Cross Road REIGERSBURG CAMP at 5.30 p.m on 11th September 1917.

From here they will guide Sub-Sections to Admirals Road and to gun position ¼ hour intervals between Sub-Sections. No. 3 Section Gun teams occupying positions 1 & 2 leading

2.

followed by gun teams occupying positions 3 & 4 and so on.

Limbers will move direct to Admirals Road and dump Guns etc leaving a guard. Teams will pick up their respective loads at Admirals Road en route to gun positions.

Guides from positions 1, 2, 3, 4 will be at No 2 Section H.Q. 2 i.e, position (7.8). at BUNT.

9. GUIDES FOR RIGHT SECTOR

Guides for No 4 Section occupying positions 9, 10, 11, 12 will be at Ration Dump along St Julien Road C 18 a 15 95 at 9 p.m. 11th Sept. Teams will be guided to above Ration Dump by guides provided by No 4. Section of 215 Coy at CHEDDAR VILLA at 8.30 p.m. Guides for Section No. 1. occupying positions 13, 14, 15, 16 will be at Cheddar Villa at 8.30 p.m. move by Sub-Sections at 1/4 hr. intervals. The teams for Right Sector may come via No 2a Bridge & Bath Track, (duck boards) leads all the way

10. INFORMATION

No. 3 Section at gun positions 1 & 2, 3 men per team under a N.C.O.

At Gun positions 3 & 4 there is accommodation for 2 Infantry Coy H.Q. M.G. Section H.Q, 3 men per team + 1. N.C.O.

Remainder of men in Section will remain at Rear H.Q and act as carrying parties for rations. Inter team reliefs will be carried out under Section arrangements with these spare men.   3.

11. COMMUNICATION

By Day Nil.

By night by runner to No. 2 Section H.Q. where they are in touch with Battalion H.Q.

No. 2 Section positions 5, 6, 7, 8.

Accommodation at 5 & 6 for 6 men only, i.e. 5 men and a N.C.O. Remainder of this Section remain at Section H.Q. at Position 7 & 8 - relief arranged under Section officer arrangement.

At position 7 & 8. 3 men per team under a N.C.O. Remainder of teams for this Sub Section at Rear H.Q. and relief arranged by Section Officers.

Communication via Battalion H.Q. in immediate vicinity.

12. DANGER POINT.

Teams are comparatively safe so long as they do not roam about.

Barrage comes down on Steenbach heavily.

13. COMPLETION OF RELIEF

By wire Code Word AXES.

There is a dump of Belt Boxes, Belts S.A.A. in vicinity of position 5 & 6.

No. 4 & 1 Section Right Sector position 9, 10, 11, 12, 13, 14, 15, 16 accommodation for 4 men + 1. N.C.O per team. Remainder at rear H.Q. Section officers H.Q. in good strong nebus.

4.

"Section Officers are responsible that French Standing Orders are read and complied with so far as is possible in the Sector.

L. J. ? Pullen
Capt
O.C 206 M.G. Co

Sept 10th 1917
Addendum 11/9/17

To Left Section
In any event relief put back, 2 hours.
If shewn on — — — — — , 4 hours

To Right Section

To Section occupying position at Cheddar Villa to be there at 8.30 sharp.
The Section going into front line will report ~~there and~~ at Cheddar Villa at 12 midnight.

Copy No 1   Brigade Office
     2   O.C 206 M.G Co.
     3   O.C. 215 M.G Co
     4   O.C Section 1
     5   "   2
     6   "   3
     7   "   4

OPERATION ORDER No. 12.

By Captain J. L. Pullar,
Commanding 206 Machine Gun Company.
September 12th, 1917

INFORMATION

The 214 Machine Gun Company will relieve the guns of 206 Company in left sector on night of 13th/14th.

No 3 Section will, on completion of relief, move into reserve at REIGERSBURG CAMP. O.C. Section will report on his way down, that relief has been properly effected, to Advanced Company Headquarters.

No. 2 Section will be relieved by Section of 214 M.G.Coy. in vicinity of OBLONG FARM, and will occupy the positions vacated by this Company.

STORES.

All stores will be handed over except Guns and Spare Parts.

GUIDES.

Guides from No. 3 Section, for gun positions 1.2.3.4, will be at the BUND at 8 pm on night of 13th, and guide incoming teams to these positions.

Guides from No. 2 Section for gun positions 5.6.7.8, will be at 2nd Bridge Head at 7.30 pm on night of 13th inst, and guide incoming teams to these positions.

On completion of relief No. 2 Section will move into positions vacated by the Section of 214 Coy.

No 1 Section will be guided to its section by guides of 2nd Company, who will be at the BUND about 9 am.

No 2 Section will report when complete by code word ~~____~~ LOCK.

                                                Captain
                                  O.C. 206 Machine Gun Coy.

OPERATION ORDER Nº 14

Copy N° 6

By Captain L.J.L. Pullar.

Commanding 206 Machine Gun Company

The attack on the enemy is to be resumed on a date to be notified later.

The Boundaries and final Objectives of Brigade are shown on attached map. POELCAPPELLE 1/10000 Edition 3

The Task allotted to the 173rd Infantry Brigade will be carried out by the 2/4th Battalion.

Tanks will co-operate.

2/2nd Battn London Regt will be relieved on night 18/19 Sept. by a Battalion of 174th Infantry Brigade.

The Machine Guns of the Division will co-operate by delivering Barrage Fire as follows:-

206 M.G. Coy	8 guns	
214	16	
215	16	
Total	40 guns	

The guns are divided into 5 ~~Battalions~~ Batteries

V. Battery	8 guns	206 M.G. Coy.
W	8	214
X	8	214
Y	8	215
Z	8	215

The location of V Battery on X.Y. night will be CANOPUS TRENCH Area C.17.b.

The location of V. Battery after moving forward
JEW HILL C.12.d.0.5.5.5

Targets are lettered to agree with the Battery engaging the target, and are numbered in order of lifts in accordance with Time Table below.

BARRAGE TABLE

Battery	Location	From	To	Target	Rate of Fire
V. L.C 206 M.G.Coy	Canopus Trench	Zero	Zero + 1 Hour	Z3	Continuous
	Upon completion i.e., at Zero + 1 hour guns will move forward to Jew Hill and open fire in accordance with Barrage Table 2.				

BARRAGE TABLE 2

Battery	Location	Lift	From	To	Target	Rate of Fire
V. L.C 206 M.G.Coy	C.12.d. 0.5 5.5	1	Zero + 2 hrs	Zero + 2 hours 10 mins	V.1	Rapid
		2	Zero + 2 hrs 10 mins	Zero + 3 hours 30 mins	V1	Continuous
		3	Zero + 3 hrs 30 mins	Onwards	V1	Bursts
			S.O.S. Lines			Rapid
	S.O.S signals - Our Aeroplanes firing Red Lights. This signal will be responded to at once by opening fire.					

BARRAGE GUNS.

Battery V. will consist of 8 guns.   Section No. 2
                                     Section No. 3.

The Battery Commander will be Sec Lieut R.W. Kemp assisted by Sec Lieut. A.E. Way.

Sec Lieut. J.R. Walker will be reserve Battery Officer at advanced Battle Headquarters at St Julien, with 6 men as reserve gunners.

CONSTRUCTION OF EMPLACEMENTS.

Gun emplacement in Canopus Trench and Forward Position must be constructed as quick as possible. No. 4. Section under Sec. Lieut. Pithouse will be responsible that the work is carried out under the direction of the Battery Commander Sec. Lieut. R.W. Kemp.

Great secrecy must be observed in the construction of the forward emplacements, and they must be camouflaged during and after construction.

No person must be allowed to approach this position by day.

T. pieces will be used in construction of emplacements.

AMMUNITION AND WATER

This Company will draw 150 boxes of S.A.A. from Divisional Dump, and this will be conveyed to Battery positions at C.12.d.05 55 on night of 17th Sept. This ammunition <u>must</u> be camouflaged or covered up.

This ammunition will be conveyed by Transport as far up the St. Julien Road as possible and conveyed from there to Battery Dump by fatigue drawn from No. 3 Section.

16 Petrol tins filled with water will be conveyed with this ammunition.

COMMUNICATION.

A double line will be run from Battery to Battle Headquarters at St. Julien. A Tape will be laid on night of 17th inst to mark forward Battery positions.

FILLED SANDBAGS

A few sandbags already filled will be left at Forward Battery position for purpose of settling down legs of tripod when gun is mounted.

CLINOMETERS.

The Battery will have 6 Clinometers and elevation should be constantly checked during fire.

COMPASS

Every Officer must make certain of the variations of his Compass.

SPARE BARRELS

The Battery Commander will see that spare barrels are available for use when required.

O.C. Coy will notify D.M.G.O. by Code word BELT when Battery positions are completed, and Map Ref. of Ammunition and Water dump sent.

Firing Chart (Form K) will be prepared and forwarded to O.C. Coy for checking and signature.

A copy of the Chart will be forwarded to D.M.G.O.

Tactical Situation Report of operations will be sent by O.C. Coy to D.M.G.O every 24 hours.

D.M.G.O.

D.H.Q. Canal Bank.

BELT FILLING CENTRES will be established in vicinity of Battery.

MOVE. Nos. 2 and 3 Sections will move into position in Canopus Trench on X.Y. night.

Copies Sent.
No. 1 O.C. 206 M.G. Coy.
No. 2 O.C. No. 2 Section
No. 3 Brigade H.Q. 173rd
No. 4 D.M.G.O.
No. 5 Lieut A.E. Way.
No. 6 War Diary

Captain,
Commanding 206 M.G. Coy.

Army Form C. 2118.

WAR DIARY
or
INTELLIGENCE SUMMARY.
(Erase heading not required.)

Place	Date	Hour	Summary of Events and Information	Remarks and references to Appendices
Autuques	1.10. 1917		Company entrained at PENELION for AUTUQUES, PAS DE CALAIS. Transport proceeded by road.	
do.	2.10. 1917		Programme of work carried out.	
do.	3.10. 1917		Programme of work carried out.	
do.	4.10. 1917		Programme of work carried out.	
do.	5.10. 1917		Programme of work carried out. 2 O.R. admitted to Hospital.	
do.	6.10. 1917		Programme of work carried out. Letter received from a Field Officer, D.A.D.Oy on Divisional Staff stating that Divisional Commander and his Staff are very pleased with the excellent work done by the Company in recent operations N.W. of Ypres.	
do.	7.10. 1917		Programme of work carried out.	
do.	8.10. 1917		Programme of work carried out. One O.R. admitted to Hospital.	
do.	9.10. 1917		Programme of work carried out.	
do.	10.10. 1917		Programme of work carried out. 2nd Lieut. T. Owen reported this day and taken on the strength of the Co.	
do.	11.10. 1917		Programme of work carried out. 2 O.R. admitted to Hospital.	
do.	12.10. 1917		Programme of work carried out. One man admitted to Hospital.	

Army Form C. 2118.

WAR DIARY
or
INTELLIGENCE SUMMARY.

(Erase heading not required.)

Instructions regarding War Diaries and Intelligence Summaries are contained in F. S. Regs., Part II. and the Staff Manual respectively. Title pages will be prepared in manuscript.

Place	Date	Hour	Summary of Events and Information	Remarks and references to Appendices
Wittinques	13 to Oct 17		Programmes of work carried out.	
	18.10.17		Programme of work carried out in morning. Company moved off in afternoon for Brigade Tactical Scheme.	
	19.10.17		Company moved off to Brigade Training Area, and took part in Brigade Tactical Scheme.	
	20.10.17		Programme of work carried out.	
	21.10.17		Programme of work carried out.	
	22.10.17		Company took part in Brigade Field Day.	
	23.10.17		Company moved off from AUTINQUES and marched to AUDRUICK, where they entrained for RIJKSBURG CAMP. The Company then proceeded to CANAL BANK, N.W. of Ypres and took over Billets. Transport proceeded by road and took over Billets and Lines at SIEGE CAMP.	
	24.10.17		Company resting.	
	25.10.17 and 26.10.17		Company relieved 54 M.G.Co in the Line and carried out operations in accordance with Operation Orders Nos 17 and 18 and Operation Report attached.	
	27.10.17		Company relieved by 214 M.G.Co who proceeded from CANAL BANK, N.W. of Ypres by 'bus to SIEGE CAMP.	
	28.10.17		Company resting.	
	29.10.17		A Battery of 4 guns were sent into the Line to assist 174 Infantry Brigade in Barrage work.	
	30.10.17		Company less Battery of 4 guns in the Line proceeded by train to ROAD CAMP Ref. Sheet 27. Belgian Transport went forward to this Camp by road. Section in Line relieved casualties 7 O.R. wounded	
	31.10.17		Company Programme	

RELIEF OPERATION ORDER. No. 17.

Copy No.

By CAPTAIN L.J.L.PULLAR,
Commanding 206. Machine Gun Company.

1. The Brigade will relieve 54th Infantry Brigade (18th Division) in the Line and take over Divisional Sector tonight 24th/25th Oct October 1917.

2. The Sector will be temporarily held as follows:-

    On Right - 2/2nd Bn.London Regiment with H.Q. at V.19.a.7.1
    On Left - 2/3rd Bn.London Regiment with H.Q. at V.19.a.7.1
    In Support - 2/4th Bn London Regiment) CANAL
                 2/1st London Regiment   ) BANK

3. 206. M.G. Company will relieve 54th M.G. Company on night 24th/25th.

Completion of relief by Code Word GRIT to O.C.

206. M.G. Company at Forward H.Q. GLOSTER FARM.

O.C. 206. M.G. Company will wire completion of relief to UPHILL, VARNA FARM by Code Word GRIT.

Relieving teams will arrive at Triangle Far U. 6. c. about 5.30 a.m. 25th October and meet guides.

The Company will move as follows:-

    Guns 1, 2, 3, and 4 move at 3.10 a.m.
    Guns 5, 9, and 10 move at 3.20 a.m.
    Guns 6, 7 and 8 move at 3.30 a.m.
    Guns 11, 12, 13, 14, 15 and 16 and H.Q. move at 3.40.a.m

Above must pass starting point, 4 Bridge at exact time.

DETAIL OF RELIEF.

No 1 and No 2 Guns, under Sec. Lieut Tomlinson will take over following positions from 54th Brigade M.G. Coy.

    1 Gun at V.14. c. 9. 5.
    1 Gun at V 14. c. 9. 6.

Nos 3 and 4 Guns, under Sec. Lieut Owen, will move with these Guns to Helles House, and will remain until time to move forward as per Operation Orders for Attack.

Nos. 5 and 9 Guns will take over positions vacated by 54th M.G. Coy as follows:-

    1 Gun at V. 20. a. 8. 2.

    1 Gun at V. 20. b. 0. 2. 0.

With these guns will move No. 10 gun, and remain at MEUNIER HOUSE until they move forward to consolidate. The guns will be under the command of Sec. Lieut Walker.

    ROUTE to Triangle via:-

        ST. JULIEN.

        POELCAPPELLE ROAD.

    STORES ETC. Nos 1, 2, 5, and 9 guns will take over from outgoing teams, Guns, Tripods, and 12 Belt Boxes per gun. Spare parts, Condensors etc will not be handed over.

    Neither blankets nor greatcoats will be taken into action.

Copies to

    No 1. O.C. Coy.
       2. Brigade H.Q.
       3. Sec.Lt. Kemp.
       4. Sec.Lt. Walker.
       5. Sec.Lt. Pithouse.
       6. Sec.Lt. Owen.

October 24th 1917.

(Sgd) L.J.L. Pullar

Captain.
Commanding 206. M.G. Company.

OPERATION ORDER No 18.

Copy No....

By CAPTAIN L. J. L. PULLAR.

Commanding 206. Machine Gun Company.

Ref. Map. Sheet:- SPRIET. 1/10000.
28 N.W. 1/20000.

----

1. (a) On a date which has been communicated verbally to those concerned, 173rd Infantry Brigade will renew the attack with 63rd Division on Right and 57th Division (XIV Corps) on the Left.

   (b) Instructions as to move etc, previous to ZERO will be found in RELIEF OPERATION ORDER No 17 attached.

2. ZERO hour will be notified later.

3. Assembly Areas, Objectives and Boundaries are shown on attached map.

   Maps shewing latest information on 1/5000 scale will be issued shortly.

   (a) The First Objective will be the DOTTED RED LINE.
   (b) The Second and Final Objective will be the SOLID RED LINE.

4. The capture and retention of high ground about PAPA FARM and WHITECHAPEL is of special importance.

5. Strong Points will be constructed as follows:-

V. 21. c. 1. 6.	by 2/2nd London Regt.
MORAY HOUSE (V. 21. c.90.65.)	" 2/2nd do.
HINTON FARM	" 2/4th do.
PAPA FARM	" 2/4th do.
CAMERON HOUSE	" 2/2nd do.
WHITECHAPEL	" 2/4th do.
V.15.a.2.2.	" 2/3rd do.
V.14.d.9.5.	" 2/3rd do.
V.14.b.6.2.	" 2/3rd do.

   Each strong point will be constructed for all round defence and to hold a garrison of one Platoon.

   A Contact Plane will fly over the Objective at ZERO plus 1 hour 30 minutes
   ZERO plus 5 hours
   and when ordered by Corps H.Q.

Each Contact Plane will be marked with TWO rectangular flags attached to and projecting from the lower plane on each side of the fuselage.

Infantry will be ready to light RED flares (in clusters of not less than three) or wave WATSON FANS if no flares are available, at the above-mentioned hour, but will not do so unless called for by KLAXON HORN or by the dropping of WHITE LIGHTS from the plane. The importance of making their position known to the Contact Planes must be impressed on all ranks.

(b) COUNTER ATTACK MACHINE. An aeroplane will be up continuously during the daylight from ZERO onwards, whose mission will be to detect the approach of enemy counter-attacks.

Whenever this patrol observes hostile parties of 100 or over moving to counter attack, it will drop a smoke bomb over that portion of the front to which the enemy is moving. The smoke bomb will burst about 100 feet below the machine into a white parachute flare which descends slowly leaving a long tail of brown smoke behind it.

7. DISPOSITION OF GUNS.

2 guns to support 2/3rd Battn, taking up positions:-
No 1 Gun at V.14. b. 3. 0. 2. 5.   Cover for spare numbers and Local Dump in Dug-out at V.14. b. 2.75. 1.25.
No 2 Gun at V. 14. d. 5. 9.   Cover for team and Local Dump in Dug-out at V. 14. d. 3. 5. 9. 25.

Both these guns will move forward to consolidate at ZERO + 40 minutes, under command of Sec. Lieut Tomlinson.

---

2 Guns to support 2/4th Battn taking up positions at
No 3 Gun at V. 15. c. 8. 25. 3. 0.

No 4 Gun at V. 15. c. 9. 0. 2. 0.
Spare numbers and Local Dump for these guns in Sub-Section Office H.Q. at V. 15. c. 8. 25. 3. 25.
These guns will move forward to consolidate at ZERO + 1 hour un Sec. Lieut. Owen

---

3 Guns to following positions:-

    No. 5 Gun.   V. 21 a. 3. 0. 8. 0.

    No. 9 Gun.   V. 21 c. 9. 0. 7. 0.

    No. 10 Gun   V. 21 c. 9. 0. 7. 0.

Move forward to consolidate at ZERO + 40 minutes under command of Sec. Lieut Walker.

----

3 guns to following positions:-

    No. 6 Gun.   V. 21 b. 3. 0. 2. 0.

    No. 7 Gun.   V. 21 b. 3. 5. 1. 25.

    No. 8 Gun.   V. 21 d. 7. 0. 8. 5.

Move forward to consolidate at ZERO + 1 hour under command of Sec. Lieut Pithouse.

    The Battery of 6 guns will deliver Overhead Barrage Fire from selected position in vicinity of V.20.c. It will assemble at GLOSTER FARM on night of 24th/25th. This Battery will fire in accordance with Firing Chart FORM K to be prepared and certified by O.C. Company, in accordance with a Barrage Time Table.

    Barrage will be in lifts of 100 yards when moving and come to rest on S.O.S. Protective Line.

    The Battery must consolidate in accordance with Operation Order No 16.

    Guns of the Battery may be called upon to reinforce the forward line.

    After the Artillery fire slackens and situation becomes normal, bursts of fire will be maintained throughout the day and night by half the Battery Guns, while the remainder are cleaned and cooled.

LINES OF FIRE will be carefully checked by constant use of clinometers. Accuracy of fire is more important than ammunition expended.

Guns Nos. 6, 7, and 8 will move to MEUNIER HOUSE and obtain guide from Infantry, thence to TRACAS FARM, where they will remain until time ordered to consolidate.

AMMUNITION BOXES.   8 Belt Boxes will be carried forward by each consolidating gun. All surplus boxes will be brought to the Local Dumps. With Battery there will be Local Dump of 100000 Rounds S.A.A and 14 Belt Boxes per Gun.

WATER FOR GUNS.   will be carried up in petrol tins to Local Dumps.

ADVANCED COMPANY H.Q. at GLOSTER FARM, to consist of

        O.C. Company.   Coy Sergeant Major
        3 Signallers   L/Cpl Knowles.
        Pte Edwards   Pte Wilson

REAR H.Q. and TRANSPORT LINES at SIEGE CAMP under Lieut Kendrick.

SITUATION REPORTS will be rendered at ZERO + 2 hours and subsequently every two hours until further orders.

    Advanced Brigade H.Q. will be at VARNA FARM (C.4. a. 5. 3.) Rear H.Q. at CANAL BANK.

    The word "RETIRE" will not be used on any account. Anyone heard using the word will be treated as an enemy and shot. This is to be explained to all ranks.

                            (Sgd) L.J.R. Pullar
                                    Captain.
October 24th 1917.   Commanding 206. Machine Gun Coy.

OPERATION REPORT.

From CAPTAIN L. J. L. PULLAR,
        Commanding 206. MACHINE GUN COMPANY.
  To H.Q.
        173rd INFANTRY BRIGADE.

      I have the honour to submit this my Report on operations of 26th October 1917.

      On 24th October I issued Relief Operation Orders (No 17) to take over following positions from 54th Infantry Brigade Machine Gun Company:-

        1 Gun at V 14. c. 9. 5.
        1 Gun at V 14. c. 9. 6.
        1 Gun at V 20. a. 8. 2.
        1 Gun at V. 20. b. 0. 2. 0.

In view of the attack to take place on morning of 26th inst I decided to move the whole of the Company into the forward area, and allot guns to various positions, which would ensure the following:-

    (1) Best Tactical Position for assembly.

    (2) Where daylight reconnaissance could be carried out on day previous to ZERO day.

DISPOSITION OF GUNS, HOLDING LINE, AND IN ASSEMBLY POSITIONS 1-16

      The guns were numbered from Left to Right before moving forward.

4 Guns and teams were ordered and moved forward to vicinity of V 14 c. 9. 5. numbered 1 to 4.

3 Guns and teams to MEUNIER HOUSE V 20 b.

3 Guns Nos 5, 9, and 10 under an Officer ordered to move forward to consolidate at Zero plus 40 minutes to following positions:-
        No 5 Gun to V 21 a. 3. 8.
        No 9 Gun to V 21 a. 9. 7.
        No 10 Gun to V 21 a. 9. 7.

These Guns to advance from MEUNIER HOUSE V 20 b.

3 Guns Nos 6, 7, and 8 under an Officer ordered to move forward to consolidate at Zero plus one hour.

These Guns to advance from Tracas Farm Post V 20 d.

6 Guns Nos 11, 12, 13, 14, 15, and 16 under 2 Officers to Barrage from prepared positions in vicinity of my H.Q GLOSTER FARM V 20 c.

Total guns in action **16.**

The relief was properly effected and assembly positions reached without casualties on night 24th/25th October.

DISPOSITION OF GUNS.
----

2 Guns Nos 1 and 2 under an Officer ordered to move forward to consolidate at Zero plus 40 to following positions:-

No 1 gun at V 14 b. 3. 2. 5.

No 2 gun at V 14 d. 5. 9.

2 Guns Nos 3 and 4 under an Officer ordered to move forward to consolidate at Zero plus 1 hour to following positions

No 3 Gun at V 15 c. 8. 25. 3. 0.

No 4 gun at V 15 c. 9. 0. 2. 0.

These guns to advance from assembly positions V 14 c. 9. 5.

An intense Barrage Fire will be delivered in accordance with Overhead Firing Chart, and on completion, fire will be maintained throughout day and night on to the S.O.S. Line in bursts at intervals.

Lines of fire and elevation will be constantly checked.

Accuracy of fire more important than rounds expended.

FOR forward guns 8 Boxes of ammunition will be carried in belts in addition to the usual loads.

INFORMATION.

The orders as detailed were carried out without a hitch with the following exceptions.

The Officer and N.C.O in advancing to Assembly position near TRACAS FARM decided to reconnoitre forward, and stumbled across about 30 of the enemy in consolidated shell holes 50 to 100 yards in front of Mebus V 31 c. 0. 25. 6. 5. The N.C.O, a Corporal, was captured. The following wire was immediately sent to Brigade notifying:-

Message No 7a
25/10/17
9.10

"To UPHILL

"Gun team reconnoitring for position near Tracas Farm. Went on to Mebus at V 21 c. 0. 6. 5. Found Mebus occupied by enemy and

about thirty in front in organised shell holes aaa.
    A N.C.O. in advance was captured by the enemy. No other losses aaa: This N.C.O. is reliable and also does not know date of operations.
                    UMBALA. H.Q. Upstart.

The following message received from UPHILL at my H.Q. and instructions immediately acted upon:-

B.M Message
25.10.17.
9.3.p.m.
           UMBALA
"Brigade on left intend to place posts on spur about V 8.d.7.7. and Brigade on right intend to occupy ground about V 22 d. 2.2. aaa   Warn guns Nos 9, 10, and 1 accordingly. "   UPHILL"

On completion of assembly UPHILL notified by Code Word "GOODELF"

At Zero the Barrage Guns, which were placed in consolidated shell holes to right of GLOSTER FARM opened intense fire and continued in accordance with Artillery Barrage Time Table.

On completion of Barrage viz:- at Zero plus 2.32 half the guns were dismounted for cleaning and cooling, and remainder continued at intervals in bursts. Rounds expended 30000.

2 tripods destroyed by shell fire during the Barrage and 3 casualties.

Shortly after Zero own Infantry on Right were seen by us advancing in good order over PAPA FARM RIDGE.

A fewwminutes after Zero the Enemy put down his Barrage on a line between TRACAS FARM and my H.Q. GLOSTER FARM.

Enemy Barrage apparently light.

UPHILL advised of this by following message:-

Message No 15.
26.10.17.
8.30.a.m.
          UPHILL Advanced.
"Barrage completed aaa Firing on S.O.S. Line in bursts at intervals aaa Estimated casualties 7 other ranks. Infantry advanced on right advanced well over PAPA FARM CREST aaa No Reports in yet from forward consolidated guns aaa A few minutes after Zero enemy barrage dropped between these H.Q. and TRACAS FARM aaa Very light Barrage. aaa   O/c UMBALA Advanced H.Q.

Information received that enemy counter attacking, and our whole line being forced back. Immediately ordered Battery to abandon S.O.S Lines, and lay out for direct protection in event of further withdrawal. One gun having been left isolated in the withdrawal moved back to MEUNIER HOUSE. I ordered another gun from Battery to reinforce it, and form a strong point. Lines of fire were laid to protect the position in conjunction with the ~~txxxx~~ remaining three guns of the Battery. The original front line was now made practically secure. These guns did not have occasion to fire, as the counter attack was repulsed by the machine guns situated near TRACAS FARM Mebus. Following message sent to Brigade:-

Message 16a UPHILL. Advanced.
26.10.17.
"Following message received from Machine Gun Officer who is at concrete mebus 21 c. 1.0.6.9 aaa MORAY HOUSE is not yet taken as previously reported by 2/2nd Battn Snipers and machine guns are very active aaa The machine guns appear to be in the vicinity of CAMERON HOUSE aaa Communication not yet established with No 5 gun aaa The three gun teams sent forward to support 2/4th are intact and in position at this Mebus to resist counter attack aaa News has just arrived that enemy are counter attacking aaa Have laid part of Battery for defensive measures aaa   O/c UMBALA.

I ordered the 3 guns which should have consolidated final objective to remain at TRACAS FARM Mebus with the three guns detailed to this place in order to form a very strong point.

These guns under 2nd Lieut J.R.Walker and 2nd Lieut W. Pithouse repulsed the counter attack and fired at several attempts to form a line, and dispersed an attempt to collect for another counter attack. I tried to establish communication with my No 5 gun, which should have consolidated at V 21 a. 3. 8. but could not do so.

One gun outside TRACAS FARM Mebus was damaged by a shell splinter, so 4 guns in action there: one inside mebus in reserve.
Following message wired to Brigade:-

Message No 17 UPHILL
26.10.17.
" There are five machine guns in action at V 21 c. 1.0.6.0 Our Infantry on right are again attacking aaa At earliest moment three guns will move further forward aaa I have ordered one gun and team from the Battery to Meunier House for defence aaa My Section Officer reports Cameron House not in our hands aaa
UMBALA Advanced.

Following message sent to UPHILL at 11.22 a.m.:-

Message No 19a UPHILL
26.10.17.
Machine Gun Officer at TRACAS FARM Mebus V 21 c.1.0.6.0. reports counter attack made against this position at 9 a.m. aaa This was repulsed by two machine guns aaa Four guns are now in action at this position mounted ready for counter attack aaa I am sending up ammunition to this position drawing from Bulow Dump"
Umbala. Advanced.

At 11.30 established communication with 214 Machine Gun Co and notified them that we were holding the line BEEK HOUSES -- TRACAS FARM MEBUS, MEUVIER HOUSE and asked them for news of the line held by us between Mebus V 20 a 1. 8. and MEUNIER HOUSE.

Following message wired to UPHILL 12.5.

Message No 23a
26.10.17.

UPHILL

" Report from Section Officer attached to 2/3rd Battn
"Went over top to previously selected positions at Zero plus 40 and dug in. At about Zero plus 100 Infantry retired beyond previously held positions. Held out in forward positions to Zero plus 115 and then retired by four bounds on to original position at intervals of 15 minutes. Have managed to gather 1/2 platoon of Infantry and have formed a small strong point at V 14 c. 9. 5. All rations lost. No news of Sub-Section under Mr Owen"

UMBALA, Advanced.

Following message sent to my Officer on Left Sector at 12.25

Message No 24a
26.10.17.

Sec. Lieut TOMLINSON.

UMBALA

"Your message received aaa Can you find out what has happened to Owen and any other information regarding troops between REQUETE FARM - HELLES HOUSE - NOBLES FARM. We hold line from BEEK HOUSES - TRACAS FARM MEBUS - MEUNIER HOUSE trying to establish touch between MEUNIER HOUSE - NOBLES FARM aaa Message received from Isaacs 214 Coy states that he occupies Mebus V 20 a. 1. 8. aaa Please reply by bearer aaa

UMBALA Advanced.

Reply received as follows:-

Message
"B" 26.10.17.

To UMBALA

From O/c No 1 Section.

"Both my teams and myself are at present occupying shell hole positions roughly V 14 c. 9. 5 and V 14 c 9. 6.

The Infantry are well in rear of this point.
As far as we know we are 200 yards in advance of them.
I have had no news of Mr Owen or teams.

Situation remained unchanged throughout day.

Total casualties 53 Other Ranks.

7 Killed
1 Missing
1 Prisoner of War.
44 Wounded.

Relieved by 214 Machine Gun Company.
Relief completed 6 a.m. 27th October 1917.

I have the honour to be,
Your obedient servant,

B.E.F.

(Sgd)
Captain.

27th Oct 1917.

S U P P L E M E N T A R Y   T O

O P E R A T I O N   R E P O R T.

The following was omitted from Operation Report:-

About 10 a.m. a party of 3 horsemen appeared in direction of CAMERON HOUSE about 300 yards from the TRACAS FARM Mebus. The Machine Guns here immediately opened fire and apparently destroyed them for they fell.

(Sgd) R. J. L. Pallor
Captain.

B. E. F.

27th October 1917.

Army Form C. 2118.

WAR DIARY
INTELLIGENCE SUMMARY
(Erase heading not required.)

Instructions regarding War Diaries and Intelligence Summaries are contained in F. S. Regs., Part II. and the Staff Manual respectively. Title Pages will be prepared in manuscript.

Place	Date	Hour	Summary of Events and Information	Remarks and references to Appendices
ROAD CAMP PROVEN AREA.	1917 Nov. 1st		Company carried out programme of work. One Other Rank rejoined from Hospital. One Other Rank proceeded to Course of Instruction at G.H.Q. School.	
	2nd		Programme of work carried out.	
	3rd		Programme of work carried out. A reinforcement of 50 Other Ranks joined from Base Depot.	
	4th		Programme of work carried out.	
	5th		Programme of work carried out. 20 Other Ranks joined from Base Depot.	
	6th		Company and First Line Transport moved by road to S. Camp. Map. Ref. Sheet 28, A.16 as per Operation Order No 20 attached.	
S. CAMP	7th		Programme of work carried out.	
	8th		do. do. do.	
	9th		do. do. do. One Other Rank joined. Company from Base Depot.	
	10th to 13th		Company relieved 214.M.G.Co in the Line in accordance with Operation Order No 21. and Section Reliefs effected as in Operation Order No 22 attached. Operations carried out as per Reports dated 11th, 12th, and 13th November 1917 attached.	
	14th		Personnel at advanced H.Q. CANAL BANK moved to Rear H.Q. SIEGE CAMP.	

Army Form C. 2118.

WAR DIARY
or
INTELLIGENCE SUMMARY

(Erase heading not required.)

Instructions regarding War Diaries and Intelligence Summaries are contained in F. S. Regs., Part II. and the Staff Manual respectively. Title Pages will be prepared in manuscript.

Place	Date	Hour	Summary of Events and Information	Remarks and references to Appendices
	1917 Nov			
	15th		Three Sections plus H.Q. and Transport of Company moved to PLAISTOW CAMP, PROVEN AREA, as detailed in Operation Order No 23 attached.	
PROVEN	16th		Programme of work carried out. Section in Line relieved 241 M.G.Co, and proceeded to SIEGE CAMP.	
	17th		Programme of work carried out. Section left SIEGE CAMP and moved to PLAISTOW CAMP to join the Company.	
	18th		Programme of work carried out.	
	19th		do. do. One Other Rank admitted to Hospital.	
	20th		Programme of work carried out.	
	21st		Programme of work carried out. 10 Other Ranks transferred to 198 M.G.Co, and 12 Other Ranks transferred to 215 M.G.Co	
	22nd		Programme of work carried out.	
	23rd		do. do.	
	24th		do. do. One O.R admitted to Hospital.	
	25/26th		Company moved to BRUNEMBERT as per Operation Order No 24 attached.	
BRUNEMBERT	27th		Programme of work carried out.	
	28th		Programme of work carried out.	
	29th		Programme of work carried out.	
	30th		Programme of work carried out.	

OPERATION ORDER. No. 20.

Copy No. 6

By CAPTAIN L. J. L. PULLAR,
Commanding, 206. Machine Gun Company.

REVEILLE   5.a.m.
BREAKFAST   6.a.m.
COMPANY PARADE   9.a.m.   MOVE OFF 9.25.a.m.

MOVE.

The Company will move by road, NORTH SWITCH ROAD S. A.26. b :- Military Road to Camp in A.16 (Sheet 28), passing starting point - Brigade Headquarters at 9.30.a.m.

FIRST LINE TRANSPORT will move in rear of Company passing starting Point at 9.45 a.m.

BRIGADE HEADQUARTERS. closes ROAD CAMP 8.45.a.m.; Opens BRAKE CAMP 8.45.a.m. 6th inst.

ADVANCE PARTY. An Advance Party of 2 N.C.O's and L/Corporals Knowles and Chisholm and 4 Officers' Servants under 2nd Lieut. Watkins to report to Area Commandant, S.CAMP to take over Camp and Transport Lines.

2nd Lieut Watkins and L/Corporal Pearson will move off on horseback at 7 a.m, and report to Area Commandant immediately on arrival.

The remainder of the billeting party will move off with motor lorry.

The Orderly Corporal will take over Lorry at Brigade H.Q. at 7. a.m., 6th inst.

The Lorry will contain:-
(1) Quartermaster's Stores.
(2) Officers' Kits.
(3) Blankets rolled in bundles of ten.
(4) Orderly Room Stores.

Rear Party.

A rear party of one N.C.O and 6 men will be detailed by C.S.M., to remain behind at ROAD CAMP and clean up.

A certificate will be obtained from Camp Adjutant

that the Camp has been left in a clean and sanitary condition.

This party will move off to S Camp on completion, and hand the certificate to O/c Company on arrival.

Section Officers will detail brakesmen for limbers.

RATIONS for 7th inst will be issued in new area.

DRESS Full marching order with Steel Helmets, less packs which will be carried on Section Limbers.

                         Captain.
                 Commanding 206. Machine Gun Co.

Copies to:-
- No 1. O.C. 206. M.G.Co.
- 2. Adjutant.
- 3. Section Officers.
- 4. C.S.M.
- 5. Transport Officer.
- 6. War Diary.

November 5th 1917.

OPERATION ORDER. No. 21.

Copy No...

By CAPTAIN. L.J.L.PULLAR.
Commanding 206. Machine Gun Company.

REF. MAP. - POELCAPPELLE 1/10000.

RELIEF.

The 206th Machine Gun Company will relieve the 214th Machine Gun Company in the Line on night of the 10th/11th November 1917, and on completion, O.C. Company will be notified by Code Word CRABS.

DISPOSITION.

2 Guns in vicinity of Battalion H.Q. at V 19 a. 6. 0. 2. 0.
2 Guns in vicinity of Trench V 19. 1. 5. 5. 3. 5.

OBJECT.

These Guns are placed for purpose of Harassing Fire on to Enemy. Fire Chart containing Targets etc will be handed over by 214 Machine Gun Company. From the Targets given the calculations must be independently checked by O.C. Battery before fire is opened

O.C. Company will be notified that this has been done by Code Word WHALES.

Guns will be dismounted by day with exception of one gun at V 19 a. 6. 0. 2. 0, which will be used for Anti- Aircraft work.

EMPLACEMENTS AND DUG OUT.

Will be constructed where necessary in accordance with training instructions.

REPORTS AND CASUALTY RETURNS

Will be sent to O.C. Company at his H.Q, through Battalion H.Q. in accordance with Trench Standing Orders.

DETAIL.

One Section = 4 Guns consisting of 4 men per gun team will be drawn as follows:-

2 Gun Teams from No 3. Section under 2nd Lieut T. Owen and

Sergeant Clarkson for position in Trench V 19 d 5.5.3.5.

2 Gun Teams from No 4 Section under 2nd Lieut Pithouse and Sergeant Shepherd at position V 19 a. 6.0. 2.0.

STORES

Outgoing teams will hand over Guns, Tripods and Belt Boxes, but not First Aid Cases. The Stores to be handed over will be carefully checked and deficiencies noted on receipt given. Belt Boxes being Divisional Reserve no receipt for same will be given but number taken over will be carefully checked and O.C.Company notified for purpose of advising Division. These will be checked again upon relief and deficiencies noted.

2 Tripods will be handed over by 214 M.G.Co at the Batt.H.Q. at V 19 a. 6.0. 2.0. to 2nd Lieut W. Pithouse and 2 at V 19 d. 5.5. 3.5. to 2nd T.Owen for use in his position.

MOVE

The Line Section and carrying party will move off from present H.Q. to the Line in time to arrive at the Guide Point at 2.a.m. 11th November 1917.

The usual interval will be maintained between Sub-Sections upon entering forward area.

CARRYING PARTY.

Consisting of 10 men under a N.C.O to be detailed by the Sergeant Major will move off with Section and proceed to GLOSTER FARM for the purpose of collecting 3 Guns and 2 Tripods. A guide from 214 Coy will meet the party to indicate position of these Stores at place where Duck Walk Track joins POELCAPPELLE ROAD at 2 a.m. 11th November 1917.

These Stores will be returned to Rear H.Q. and a report made to O.C. Company regarding their condition.

GUIDES

Guides from 214 Coy from both Line positions will be at bottom of Duck Board Track joining POELCAPPELLE ROAD at 2.a.m. 11th inst.

TRANSPORT

2 Limbered Wagons will convey Teams, Rations etc under arrangements made by Transport Officer.

One Limbered Wagon will await carrying party with salved guns etc as far up the ST JULIEN - POELCAPPELLE ROAD as possible and convey to Rear H.Q.

REAR H.Q. AND TRANSPORT.

Will move on 11th inst to SIEGE CAMP and take over Transport Lines and Billets from the Rear H.Q. of 214 M.G.Coy.

Time of relief 16 hours.

Rear H.Q. will consist of Nos 1 and 2 Sections, under 2nd in Command with Transport Officer and 2nd Lieut Walker, plus the reserve personnel of Company.

COMPANY H.Q.

Will be taken over from O.C.214. M.G.Coy at 16 hours 10th inst by 2nd Lieut Kemp, and will consist of details issued separately.

The Billets now occupied by 214 M.G.Coy on CANAL BANK will be taken over by remaining Sub-Sections of Nos 3 and 4 Sections under the command of 2nd Lieut A.E.Way at 16 hours 10th inst.

Copies to:-
No. 1. O.C. 206.M.G.Co.
    2. 173rd Infantry Brigade.
    3. D.M.G.O.
    4. O.C. 214. M.G.Co.
    5. Battery Commander.
    6. War Diary.

Captain.

November 10th 1917.   Commanding 206. Machine Gun Co.

OPERATION ORDER No 22.

Copy No...5.

By CAPTAIN L.J.L.PULLAR.

Commanding 206. Machine Gun Company.

INTER SECTION RELIEF.

The Gun Teams in the Line will be relieved on the night of the 12/13th by the Teams occupying Billets on the CANAL BANK.

N.C.O's.

Corporal McAteer. J. and Corporal Bolton J. will relieve
Sergeant Clarkson. H.
and Sergeant Shepherd D.

respectively.

These N.C.O's will report to the Sergeant Major on the CANAL BANK, Billet No.32, with the two Limbered Wagons at 11.30.p.m. on the 12th inst.

RATIONS AND TRANSPORT.

Rations for 48 hours will be carried to the Line with Teams, - 22 all Ranks.

2 Petrol Tins, containing Cold Tea will be included with Rations, and Tommy Cookers and Whale Oil.

One Limbered Wagon will remain at Cross Roads, St.JULIEN, and carry out relieved teams.

GUIDES.

Duck Board Track, GLOSTER FARM, POELCAPPELLE ROAD, 2.a.m. 13th inst.

RELIEVED TEAMS.

Will proceed direct to Rear H.Q, SIEGE CAMP.

Salved Guns and Stores, if any, will be carried to Rear H.Q and condition reported upon.

GUN OIL AND FLANNELLETTE.

will be sent up with this party to each position.

On completion of Relief O.C.206 Machine Gun Company will be notified by Code Word LIMPETS.

Copy No 1. 173rd Infantry Brigade H.Q.
      2. O.C. 206. M.G.Co.
      3. Battery Commander.
      4. Adjutant. 206.M.G.Co.
      5. War Diary.

November 11th 1917.

                                                Captain.
                              Commanding 206.Machine Gun Co.

REPORT. ref Operations No 21.22

Copy No. 4

To D. M. G. O.
    58th DIVISION.

From OFFICER COMMANDING, 206. Machine Gun Co.

I received Operation Order No. 110 dated 9th November 1917 at 20 hours on 11th, therefore too late to comply with paragraphs 5, 6, and 7.

Reference your Order No 112. of 10th November 1917 to search for Vickers Guns and Material dumped near Left Battalion H.Q. at V 19 a. 6.0. 2.0., this has been complied with and nothing can be found.

Reference Divisional Reserve Belt Boxes, I have 172 as follows:-

    135 at V 19 a. 6.0. 2.0.
    37 at V 20 c. 4.3.

DISPOSITION OF GUNS.

Map reference of GLOSTER FARM gun positions:-

    V 20 c. 4.0. 3.0. = 2 Guns

LEFT BATTALION H.Q. gun positions:-

    V 19 a. 6.0. 2.0. = 2 Guns

Am relieving teams tonight as per Operation Order No 22.

SITUATION.

Situation quiet and casualties NIL.

----

214 Machine Gun Company have not yet complied with your Order, N 5, dated 3rd November 1917, to hand over five guns and eight tripods.

They have handed over 2 guns only at GLOSTER FARM instead of 3 guns and 2 tripods.

The following stores are required from 214. Machine Gun Company to replace those handed over on relief after the operations of 26th/27th October 1917:-

        3 Guns.
        8 Tripods.
        7 First Aid Cases.
        1 Condenser Bag.
        28 Belts and Belt Boxes.

May this matter be settled without further delay please?

I suggest that it be done as follows:-

Upon this Company being relieved, the gun deficiency viz:- three, be made up from the 4 guns now in the Line, thus I will return to 214. Machine Gun Company one gun only.

The Tripod Deficiency viz:- Eight. I will retain possession of the four in the Line, which will reduce the deficiency to four, the 214 Machine Gun Company handing over to me at their Rear H.Q. this deficiency.

The Seven First Aid Cases and the Condenser Bag were handed over to 214.M.G.Co, and receipt obtained, so these to be replaced at Rear H.Q. by them with the 4 tripods.

Belt and Belt Box Deficiency = 28, handed over and receipt obtained. These to be drawn from Divisional Reserve in Line, and carried out by us on our relief.

Will you please advise me, whether this arrangement is satisfactory to you and can be ordered, for it is essential that I am made up to full fighting strength without delay, otherwise I must render a full report to my Brigade.

        I have the honour to be,

        Your obedient servant,

November 12th 1917.
        Captain.
        Commanding 206.M.G.Co.

Copy No 1. D.M.G.O.
      2. O.C. M.G.Co. 206
      3. 173.Infantry Brigade.
      4. War Diary.

FORM G.2.   No.1.

DAILY REPORT (see Nos 21, 22,)
ON
FIRING.
WORK DONE.
INTELLIGENCE SUMMARY.
TACTICAL SITUATION.

BATTERY I.   206. MACHINE GUN CO.

Time and Date	No. of Gun.	Map Ref. Gun Fired.	Times of Firing	Target.	Rounds Fired	Work Done	Intelligence Summary
From 2.a.m. 11.11.17 to 2.a.m. 12.11.17	1 x	V.19.a. 6.0.2.0.	Intervals during night.	Papa Farm. V 21 b. 1.0.3.5	3000	Improved Positions	Situation quiet. Casualties Nil.
do	2	do.	do.	Hilton Farm	3000	do.	
do	1 x	----	----	----	----	----	
do	3 x	V.20.c. 4.0.3.0.	----	V 22 a. 4.5.4.2 to V 22 a. 4.2.6.0.	----	Improved Positions	do.
do.	4.	do.	----	V 22 a. 0.3.8.5 to V 22 a. 1.0.6.2.	----	do.	do.
	3 x	----	----	----	----	----	

x = Anti-aircraft by day

TACTICAL SITUATION REPORT.

Intermittent shelling throughout night, mostly 100 yards in front of MEBUS V 19 a. 6.0. 2.0., chiefly 5.9s. Duck Walk track from MEBUS to POELCAPPELLE ROAD, also shelled at intervals by day, but heavily shelled from 10.30.p.m to 12.0., and from 1 a.m. to 3.a.m. - 5.9s and Gas shells. Intermittent shelling throughout night in vicinity of GLOSTER FARM and Duck Walk track.

J.L. Pillar
Captain.
O.C. 206.Machine Gun Co.
173.Infantry Brigade.

FORM G.2.   No_2.

DAILY REPORT.
ON.
FIRING.
WORK DONE.
INTELLIGENCE SUMMARY.
TACTICAL SITUATION.

BATTERY I.   206. MACHINE GUN CO.

Time and Date	No. of Gun.	Map Ref. Gun Fired.	Times of Firing.	Target.	Rounds Fired.	Work Done	Intelligence Summary
From 2.a.m 12.11.17 to 2.a.m 13.11.17	1.	V 19 a. 6.0.2.0	Intervals during night	PAPA FARM V 21 b. 10.35.	2000 500 at E.A. at 2 to 4 p.m. 12.11.17	Improved Position	Situation quiet. Casualties Nil
	2.	do.	do.	HIATON FARM V 21 b. 5.2.	2000	do.	do.
	3.	V 20 c. 40.30.	------	V 22 a. 45.42. to V 22 a. 42.60.	------	do.	do.
	4.	do.	------	V 22 a. 03.85. to V 22 a. 10.62.	------	do.	do.

TACTICAL SITUATION REPORT.

Very quiet during day; a little shelling in vicinity of MEBUS V 19 a. 60. 20 at 4 p.m. From 10.30.p.m to 2.0.am. intermittent shelling in vicinity of MEBUS and Duck Walk track to POELCAPPELLE ROAD.

E.A. very active from 2 to 4.p.m. flying low over front line posts.

New Fire Targets (2 per Battery) with calculations and S.O.S. Lines forwarded to Battery 12th/13th November 1917.

L. J.L. Pullen
Captain.
O.C.206. Machine Gun Co.
173rd Infantry Brigade.

FORM G.2.   No 3.

DAILY REPORT.
On
FIRING
WORK DONE.
INTELLIGENCE SUMMARY.
TACTICAL SITUATION.

BATTERY 1.   206. MACHINE GUN CO.

Time and date	No of Gun	Map Ref. Gun Fired	Times of Firing	Target	Rounds Fired	Work done	Intelligence Summary
From 2 a.m 13.11.17 to 2.a.m. 14.11.17	1	V 19 a. 6.0. 2.0.	Intervals during night	G H	1000 1000	Improved my position	Situation quiet
	2	do.	do.	I	2000	do.	
	3	V 20 c. 40. 30.	------	K	NIL	do	Unsafe to fire at this Target
	4	do.	Intervals during night	A	3000	do	
	1 2 2	V 19 a. 60.20 do	4.30.p.m S.O.S.) to 5.p.m. S.O.S.)		1500	do	Received O.K from forward posts at 5.p.m.

TACTICAL SITUATION REPORT.

During night intermittent shelling on St. JULIEN and POELCAPPELLE ROAD. Enemy Artillery very active on our Batteries on ST JULIEN POELCAPPELLE ROAD, throughout the day probably owing to aerial observation of pack mules serving the Battery.

At 3.30 p.m opened on E.A. flying low near my position - 100 rounds.

Enemy fired Gas Shells in vicinity of MEUNIER HOUSE and TRACAS FARM at 4.p.m.

Captain.
Commanding 206 Machine Gun Co.
173rd Infantry Brigade.

OPERATION ORDER No. 23.

By CAPTAIN L.J.L.PULLAR.   Copy No. 5.

    Commanding 206.MACHINE GUN COMPANY.

MOVE.

    Three Sections plus Headquarters and Transport will move by road from SIEGE CAMP to PLAISTOW CAMP, PROVEN Area on the 15th inst.

STARTING POINT.

    Junction of MILITARY ROAD - PESELHOEK - WESTERN ROAD in A 16 a.

    Head of Company will pass Starting Point at 10.27.a.m.

ROUTE.

    MILITARY ROAD - INTERNATIONAL CORNER (A 9 a. 2. 4.) - MILITARY ROAD - 2 Area PROVEN.

    (F 21. Sheet 27)

ADVANCE PARTY.

    2nd Lieut Walker and L/Cpl Pearson will proceed to New Area at 8 a.m. to take over Camp, and Horse Lines.

    The Company will be met by a guide to lead to Billets.

REAR PARTY.

    Will be detailed by Sergeant Major to clean up Billets etc, obtain Certificate from the Area Commandant. This will be handed to O.C. Company upon arrival.

LORRIES.

    Corporal Bolton will report to Brigade H.Q. at BRAKE CAMP at 7 a.m. to take over Lorry.

    Blankets in bundles of ten will be carried on lorry.

    C.Q.M.S. will accompany the lorry.

BAGGAGE WAGON.

    will convey Quartermaster Sergeant's Stores to new Area, and will proceed with Transport.

H.Q.

H.Q. LIMBER.

Will carry O.C's Kit and Adjutant's, and Orderly Room Stores.

L/Cpl Knowles will be responsible for the H.Q. Limber and its contents.

DRESS.

<u>Full Marching Order.</u> Tin hat to be carried on pack.

Jerkins in Limbers.

PARADE.

7.45.a.m. Move off 8.a.m.

TRANSPORT.

Move 200 yards in rear of Unit.

MARCH DISCIPLINE.

Will be rigidly enforced and Sergeant Major will check and report any irregularities.

SALUTING G.O.C.

When passing the G.O.C. usual compliments will be paid by Officer Commanding Company.

On "Eyes Right" being ordered by Officer Commanding, every man will turn his head smartly to right, and look up towards the Officer saluted.

Copy No.1. O.C.206.M.G.Co.
    2. H.Q.173rd Infantry Brigade.
    3. O.C's 1,2,3,4 Sections.
    4. Transport.
    5. War Diary.
    6. File.

                                     Captain.
                            Commanding 206.Machine Gun Co.

<u>November 14th 1917.</u>

OPERATION ORDER. No 24.

By CAPTAIN L.J.L.PULLAR.   Copy No ..5..

Commanding 206. Machine Gun Company.

1. The Brigade will be transferred from the XIX Corps to the XVIII Corps (LUMBRES AREA).

2. Personnel will move on the 25th inst. by Train to WIZERNES thence to LUMBRES Area "A", where they will find their Transport and be billetted for night 25/26th November.

   On the 26th inst, Personnel and Transport will move to Area "C".

3. Brigade Headquarters will close at PENGE CAMP at 11 a.m. and re-open at SAMETTE at noon on the 25th inst, closing at 10. a.m. on 26th and re-opebing at CHATEAU D'ALINCTHUN at same hour.

4. SERIAL 8. 25th Nov.

   The Company will move from PROVEN to AFFRINGUES by rail and march, route from WIZERNES (Detraining Point) - SERQUES - LUMBRES - BAYENGHEM - AFFRINGUES.

5. ADMINISTRATIVE.

   Entraining Officer Captain B.J.Barton, 2/2nd London Regt. (white brassard on right arm)

   2nd Lieut Tomlinson will report to the Entraining Officer at PROVEN for instructions, at 11.30. and will take with him Entraining States in triplicate, one for himself, and two he will hand to Entraining Officer.

6. PARADE.

   The Company will parade on the road in time to move off at 11.30. for PROVEN STATION.

1.

7. **DETRAINING OFFICER (WIZERNES).**

        Lieut. S.G. ASKHAM. 2/4th London Regt.

8. **WATER CART.**

        The Water Cart will move off from this Camp at 7.a.m. and report at entrance of PENTON CAMP at 8.30.a.m. under command of Lieut J.Roberts.

9. **BLANKETS.**

        One blanket per man will be carried on man to WIZERNES from thence they will be conveyed to "A" Area by lorry.

        Second blanket per man will be rolled in bundles of ten, under supervision of C.Q.M.S..

        These will be handed over with remaining stores for conveyance by lorry direct to final area.

        2nd Lieut. T.Owen will be in command of the lorry. L/Cpl Chisholm will assist him.

        2nd Lieut Owen will ascertain from Area Commandant, LUMBRES, the location of this Unit in Area "C" i.e. Final Area.

10. **STORES.**

        Stores which cannot be carried on the lorry direct to Area "C" will be carried by train.

11. **CAMP.**

        C.S.M. will obtain a certificate from the Camp Warden that the whole Camp is left in a clean and sanitary condition

        This certificate will be handed to O.C.Company on completion of move and a copy forwarded to Brigade H.Q.

12. **MARCH DISCIPLINE.**

        March discipline will be strictly enforced.

        Section Sergeants will be held responsible.

        The C.S.M. will obtain names of men who fall out on March for any reason, and hand to O.C. Company.

        These men will be brought up for Company Orders.

13. **TRAINS.**

        Train No. 2 for this Company departs PROVEN 1.p.m. 25th inst, arrives WIZERNES 4.p.m. 25th inst.

DISTRIBUTION.

On 25th inst 206.Machine Gun Company in Area "A" viz:- AFFRINQUES.

Brigade Headquarters, SAMETTE.

On 26th inst Area "C" 206. Machine Gun Company BRUNEMBERT.

Brigade Headquarters, CHATEAU D'ALINCTHUN.

14. RAILHEAD.

From 27th inst LUMBRES.

15. TIME TABLE OF MOVE.

On 26th inst Brigade Headquarters will move from SAMETTE to CHATEAU D'ALINCTHUN leaving Camp at 10.10 a.m. route direct.

206 Machine Gun Company will leave AFFRINQUES at 10.5 a.m. to BRUNEMBERT, Route direct.

16. TRANSPORT.

Transport will move with the Company from AFFRINQUES.

Copy No. 1. O.C.206.M.G.Co.
2. 173rd Infantry Brigade.
3. Section Officers.
4. C.S.M.
5. War Diary.

November 25th, 1917.

Captain.
Commanding 206.M.G.Co.

Army Form C. 2118.

WAR DIARY
or
INTELLIGENCE SUMMARY.
(Erase heading not required.)

Instructions regarding War Diaries and Intelligence Summaries are contained in F. S. Regs., Part II. and the Staff Manual respectively. Title pages will be prepared in manuscript.

Place	Date	Hour	Summary of Events and Information	Remarks and references to Appendices
BRUNEMBERT	1/12/17		Programme of training carried out	
	2/12/17		Do	
	3/12/17		Do	
	4/12/17		Do	
	5/12/17		Do	
	6/12/17		Do	
	7/12/17		Do	
			Entrained at BALINGHEM arrived at MORTAR CAMP ELVERDINGHE	
	8/12/17		Company marched to AFFRINGUES	
	9/12/17		Company left AFFRINGUES and marched to WIZERNES and entrained for ELVERDINGHE arrived at MORTAR CAMP ELVERDINGHE at 5.p.m	
MORTAR CAMP	10/12/17		Company work. Training carried out at MORTAR CAMP.	
	11/12/17		Programme of training carried out	
	12/12/17		Do	
	13/12/17		Do	

WAR DIARY or INTELLIGENCE SUMMARY

Army Form C. 2118.

Place	Date	Hour	Summary of Events and Information	Remarks and references to Appendices
MORTAR CAMP	14.12.17	C.15 H	Company moved up to KEMPTON PARK. M.D. 2.5.F. St JULIEN 28 N.W.2 Relief of B/1 Coy 1/1 H. Transport at Company reserve at MORTAR CAMP	
KEMPTON PARK	15.12.17		Company relieved 2/14 Bastings M.G. Coy. on the line. 2 5 Sections Being with no. 162 & 163 Coys. Northern Area viz :- 2 Guns at TRIANGLE FARM (1 Gun at BREWERY 1 Gun at BREWERY NORTH, 1 Gun at HELLES HOUSE and 1 Gun at N-W-E-S FARM. Four Guns were allotted to Coys Defensive Scheme :- Barrage at X.25.C.9.2. firing at 25.40 DPG 1 Gun in vicinity of DELTA HOUSE, 1 Gun in vicinity V.30 d.1.9 and 1 Gun in vicinity of V.25.C.8.2. Bay. Ref. Sheet 20 S.E. 1/20,000, St at 1.9 N.E. 1/5,000, Sheet 20 N.W. Relief effected without casualties.	
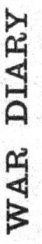	16.12.17		Enemy shelled PHEASANT FARM and PHEASANT TRENCH intermittently between 11.30 a.m. and 12.30 p.m. POELCAPELLE - ST JULIEN ROAD subjected to H.E. and H.V. Shelling from about 11.40 a.m. to 12.45 a.m. Two of our flying aircraft came down to-day. Wind N.E. - Snow view observed. Casualties NIL	
	17.12.17		Enemy light shelled forward positions camp at 6.6 a.m. Shell activity quiet during day. Enemy aircraft were fairly active. Wind N.E. Casualties NIL.	
	18.12.17		O.C. of Guns in Coys Defensive Scheme made a reconnaissance of ground about B 2nd C gone although visibility very good, confirmed little or no sign/fd day. POELCAPELLE - ST JULIEN RD from V.30.d.3.4 to C.6.C.1.2 subjected to shelling from about 3.45 p.m. to 4.30 p.m. Barrage while dry in vicinity of no. 18 farm. Barrage about 9 road Welhington 1 man killed by H.E. and H.V. Ch. E.A. [___] enemy aeroplane in flames Plane fell near ST JULIEN. Visibility Casualties NIL	

WAR DIARY or INTELLIGENCE SUMMARY

Army Form C. 2118.

Place	Date	Hour	Summary of Events and Information	Remarks and references to Appendices
	19/12/17		Enemy Countery during day fairly quiet. Vicinity of BREWERY and BREWERY NORTH shelled between 10 and 11.30 p.m. with about 100 H.E. MEUNIER HOUSE also shelled during day. Own artillery placed a barrage between 7 p.m. and 9.10 p.m. on right Enemy Machine Gun located at V.14.d.5.0.&.0. Wind Easterly Casualties One other Rank wounded. Inter section Reliefs carried out without casualties.	
	20/12/17		Enemy shelled POELCAPPELLE area intermittently between 2 p.m. and 3 p.m. Own artillery quiet. Weather misty. Casualties One other Rank wounded.	
	21/12/17		Enemy artillery active MEUNIER HOUSE shelled from 3 a.m to 6 a.m. Vicinity of POELCAPPELLE ROAD from 1 p.m to 2 p.m. Many shells hang either gas or duds. Casualties one other Rank wounded.	
	22/12/17		Hostile Artillery active. Between 4 p.m. and 5 p.m. POELCAPPELLE ROAD received a number of gas shells. Tracks from GLOSTER FARM to MEUNIER HOUSE heavily shelled from 5 to 6.30 p.m. Our artillery active at night. Wind N.E. Casualties Nil. Enemy put down barrage at 4.20 p.m. S.O.S. went up. Our artillery replied slowly.	
	23/12/17		Very quiet all day. Atmosphere rather misty. 2 sections of Machine Gun Co. and upon relief proceeded to CANAL BANK. 2 sections in the line relieved by 21st. Remainder of Battalion at KEMPTON PARK took over billets at CANAL BANK.	
	24/12/17 to 30/12/17		Programme of training carried out Company in Divisional Reserve on Canal Bank.	
	31/12/17		Company relieved by 21st Machine Gun Co. in the line. Relief effected without casualties. B Co allotted to forward positions & guns in Coy. Defensive line. Balance of personnel proceed to KEMPTON PARK and took over billets vacated by 21st M.G Co.	

WAR DIARY
INTELLIGENCE SUMMARY

Army Form C. 2118.

No. 206

Place	Date	Hour	Summary of Events and Information	Remarks and references to Appendices
	1/1/18		Company relieved 215 MACHINE GUN Co. in the line taking over 5 forward Gun positions and 4 Gun positions in Corps Defensive System. Relief effected without casualties	
	2/1/18		Front generally quiet - very little hostile shelling. Enemy aeroplane active at intervals during day. Casualties nil.	
	3/1/18		Enemy artillery inactive. PHEASANT TRENCH slightly shelled in vicinity of Coy H.Q. 5 aeroplanes fired at from HELLES HOUSE and driven off. Casualties nil.	
	4/1/18		ST JULIEN - LANGEMARCK ROAD shelled continuously during afternoon & evening. Aerial activity - quiet. Casualties Nil.	
	5/1/18		Artillery on both sides very quiet. No enemy aircraft seen. Casualties Nil.	
	6/1/18		Own artillery very active during day. Enemy shelling normal. Hostile machine gun very active from direction of MORAY HOUSE. Casualties nil.	
	7/1/18		Enemy artillery normal and front very quiet. Mine exploded at KEMPTON PARK and did some material damage to Huts in Camp. Casualties one O.R. wounded as result of this explosion	
	8/1/18		Company relieved by 106 MACHINE GUN Co., and upon completion of relief proceeded to SOLFERINO CAMP. Casualties nil	
	9/1/18		Company moved from SOLFERINO CAMP to SCHOOL CAMP - PROVEN AREA. Personnel by rail and transport by road.	
	10/1/18		Company generally cleaning and checking Guns & Stores.	

WAR DIARY
or
INTELLIGENCE SUMMARY

Army Form C. 2118.

(Erase heading not required.)

Place	Date	Hour	Summary of Events and Information	Remarks and references to Appendices
	11/1/18		Programme of Training carried out.	
	12/1/18		Brigade inspected by G.O.C. 2nd Corps. Programme of Work carried out 32 O.R. represented the Company at inspection.	
	13/1/18 to 20/1/18		Programme of Work carried out. G.O.C. Division lectured to all officers at TUNNELLING CAMP (15.1.18) on the "Principles of Defence".	
	21/1/18		Divisional transferred from II Corps to III Corps V. Army. Company entrained at PROVEN for rear areas.	
CACHY	22/1/18		Company detrained at VILLERS-BRETONNEUX and proceeded to CACHY and took over billets.	
"	23/1/18		Programme of Work carried out	
"	24/1/18		do	
"	25/1/18		do	
"	26/1/18		do	
"	27/1/18		do	
"	28/1/18		Practical Tactical Scheme carried out	
"	29/1/18		Programme of Work carried out	
"	30/1/18		do	
"	31/1/18		Practical Tactical Scheme carried out.	

Army Form C. 2118.

WAR DIARY
or
INTELLIGENCE SUMMARY.
(Erase heading not required.)

Instructions regarding War Diaries and Intelligence Summaries are contained in F. S. Regs., Part II. and the Staff Manual respectively. Title pages will be prepared in manuscript.

206 M&G Coy

Vol 1/2

Place	Date	Hour	Summary of Events and Information	Remarks and references to Appendices
	1918 Feb 1		Company in rest at CACHY. Programme of Training carried out	
	Feb 2		Officers carried out Tactical Scheme.	
	Feb 3 to Feb 6		Programme of Training carried out.	
	Feb 7		Company entrained at VILLERS BRETONNEUX, detrained at APILLY. Moved by bus from APILLY to VIRY NOUREUIL, and marched to NOUREUIL	
	Feb 8		Company relieved 89 M.G. Coy in the line, taking over 11 gun positions. Remaining 5 Guns in reserve at NOUREUIL	
	Feb 9 to Feb 16		Company engaged preparing a Defence Scheme for the LA FERE sector of the Divisional Front. During this period the enemy only shelled localities where movement was observed. Owing to the tactical situation of ground held by us and the predominating situation of the enemy and the direction of possible hostile attack the decision in selecting guns was very difficult. From the completion of the final Defence Scheme involved considerable work. Casualties - N.C.

WAR DIARY or INTELLIGENCE SUMMARY

Army Form C. 2118.

Place	Date 1916	Hour	Summary of Events and Information	Remarks and references to Appendices
	Feb 17 to Feb 28		Gun teams were detailed to commence work on position originally selected. Owing to the nature of the ground it was found necessary to abandon work on certain positions, and the services of the Royal Engineers was necessary to complete the structure and change of base positions. We decided at the commencement to build such gun positions and have done so far as possible, but so have left the building of dug outs for the accommodation of gunteams to the superior knowledge of the R.E.'s, much construction during the C or O.C's inter-sections/reliefs taken carried out as far as possible. Company Headquarters up to Feb 23rd from Feb 23rd to Feb 26th at T.16.c.00.90 were at T.27.b.65.90 (Aylmers 65 S.W.) and from Feb 26th and from Feb 26th at T.9.d.20.20. Rear Company Headquarters moved on Feb 28th from A.16.d.8.22 (1000 NW to A.10.c.65.25. Casualties, Nil.	
	Feb 16		Lieut V. M. Kendrick, 2nd in Command, left the Company for the purpose of interviewing the Indian Army Commandant. No official communication received as to the result of the interview.	

www.ingramcontent.com/pod-product-compliance
Lightning Source LLC
Chambersburg PA
CBHW081424160426
43193CB00013B/2185